Islamic Radicalism and
Anti-Americanism in Indonesia:
The Role of the Internet

Contents

List of Acronyms

BBC	British Broadcasting Corporation
CIA	Central Intelligence Agency
CNN	Cable News Network
FBI	Front Pembela Islam (the Defender of Islam Front)
FKAWJ	Forum Komunikasi Ahlus Sunnah wal Jamaah (Communications Forum of the Followers of Sunnah)
FLA	*Fiqih Lintas Agama* (Cross-Religion Fikh)
GPM	Gereja Protestan Maluku (the Protestant Church of the Maluku)
ICT	Information and Communications Technology
ITB	Institut Teknologi Bandung (Bandung Institute of Technology)
JIL	Jaringan Islam Liberal (the Islam Liberal Network)
KMNU	Kaum Muda Nahdlatul Ulama (The Youth of Nahdlatul Ulama)
KTP	*Kartu Tanda Penduduk* (Identity Card)

LSI	Lembaga Survey Indonesia (the Indonesian Survey Institute)
MI5	Military Intelligence Five
MMI	Majelis Mujahidin Indonesia (the Indonesian Mujaheeden Council)
PKS	Partai Keadilan Sejahtera (the Justice and Prosperity Party)
RMS	Republik Maluku Selatan (the South Maluku Republic)
TNI	Tentara National Indonesia (Indonesia's National Armed Forces)
UGM	Universitas Gajah Mada (Gajah Mada University)
WTC	World Trade Center

Executive Summary

This study uses Indonesia as a local site for examining how the technology and nature of the Internet interact with political and cultural struggles. It also shows how the creation and assertion of identity on the Internet become a focal point of contests over power. Specifically, the study examines the role of the Internet in Indonesia in disseminating the message of radical fundamentalist Islamic groups and, in particular, their anti-Americanism. It argues that the Internet serves as a key tool of self-definition and collective action for these groups—it communicates the *global* identity of radical fundamentalism as a means of self-definition for *local* Islamic fundamentalist movements. Two case studies detail these phenomena. The first examines Internet use by Laskar Jihad, the radical militia group involved in the Maluku conflict. The second looks at how radical fundamentalist Islamic groups have used the Internet after 9/11 to disseminate charges that the United States and Israel are conspiring against Islam. By examining how information flowed from cyberspace to real space in both cases, this study shows that the Internet has potential as a site for the revival of primordial, ethno/religious, and communal identities as forms of resistance to domination by both "non-believers" and global actors such as the United States.

Deploying the concepts of identity politics, meta-narratives, and collective action, the study examines how the Internet is used by Islamic radical-fundamentalist individuals and groups. It shows that the Internet plays a crucial yet indeterminate role in the milieus of politics, culture, and economic structure. In the case of Indonesia, the Internet has played a key role in creating and sustaining political legitimation, resistance, and identity projects among Islamic radical fundamentalists. It has also helped these groups transform their identity into social and political power capable of scaling up social responses to effect political transformations at national and global levels. The Internet is becoming a major factor in identity formation—one that can allow users to access global sources of information while interpreting that information in local identity contexts through key nodes and sources.

Indeed, Islamic radical fundamentalism has shown that the Internet has the potential to facilitate identity formation—such as the global fundamentalist movement—that is not territorially bound. But this development does not mean that national and other local identities have become obsolete in cyberspace. The Internet facilitates multiple identities: It can strengthen national identity while also fostering a de-territorialized identity. Radical fundamentalist groups also use the Internet to bypass local/national authorities and, in so doing, establish a new de-territorialized pattern of hierarchy. In addition, the ways these groups use the Internet demonstrate a mass nature that dovetails with the reductionist tendency and simplicity of the meta-narratives and more specific narratives of conspiracy these groups endorse. This resonance between the Internet and reductionism explains how the Internet can greatly facilitate the dissemination of radical fundamentalist ideas and opinions.

However, in a country such as Indonesia, in which most of the population is not yet connected to the Internet, the Internet also needs to be explicitly linked to other media in order to extend its influence. Using the intermodalities of media networks, various individuals and groups can create linkages that allow information originating from cyberspace to reach audiences beyond the Internet. The Internet and its linkages to other media have enabled the realization of new connections. Radical groups use the Internet as a trawling tool to reach potential members at local, national, and global levels.

But the Indonesian cases also show that the Internet is not persuasive enough to mobilize people for extreme actions such as killing and murder. While the Internet helps to form and disseminate a resistance identity, it alone cannot easily transform that identity into *jihad* in the form of physical war.

Islamic Radicalism and Anti-Americanism in Indonesia:
The Role of the Internet

This study focuses on the period in contemporary Indonesian history from 1999 to 2004—a brief period marked by the emergence of a revolutionary new technology (the Internet) and of unimagined political reform and global turmoil.[1] In investigating the interplay between the Internet and society during this period, this study reveals that the dynamics of social change do not form linear pathways. Instead, these dynamics are marked by breaking points and disjunctures that have no preconceived or necessary future destinations. In the milieus of politics, culture, and economic structures, the Internet as technology plays a critical yet ultimately indeterminate role. For those people who are or perceive themselves as marginalized, the Internet provides new openings and configurations in order to scale up their movements and relate local events to global levels and scale them back down again to local levels in a manner that can empower a handful of people beyond any level previously imagined. But in a world of intensifying cyber-traffic, this sudden empowerment avoids ephemerality only to the extent to which it can tap into larger identity and political structures.

With the downfall of Suharto in May 1998, Indonesia became more democratic, but its democratic character remains immature, unstable, and weak. The new government has struggled through an extended period of legitimation crisis and has been unable to serve as a vehicle for social, political, and economic justice and security. During this period, Indonesia also witnessed the rise of Islamic radicalism movements—made up of those people who believe that Islam is under threat and that they are sanctioned to defend Islam from that threat. According to these radicals, the threat to Islam mainly comes from a global conspiracy of "Zionists-Crusaders" (Jews and Christians), with the United States and Israel as the conspiracy's global leaders. Some of these radical groups, such as *Laskar Jihad*[2] (Jihad Troopers), the *Front Pembela Islam* (the Defender of Islam Front, or FBI) and the *Laskar Mujahidin Indonesia* (the Indonesian *Mujahedeen*[3] Troopers), do not hesitate to use violence as a means to accomplish their political-religious goals.

The rise of Islamic radicalism also coincided with the post-9/11 United States "war on terror," a campaign that is perceived by these radical Islamic groups as a war against Islam and which has raised anti-Americanism in Indonesia. Gaining worldwide attention, the rise of Islamic radicalism has changed the global image of Islam in Indonesia—which for decades had been perceived as moderate and tolerant—to a religion with aggressive and bellicose elements. Although the radical strain is not dominant in Indonesia, much of the country's population is ambivalent about radical fundamentalists, tacitly allowing them sanctuary in what is often referred to as the most populous Islamic nation in the world.

While recent fundamentalist radicalism and post-9/11 anti-Americanism appear to be new developments, they are actually rooted in long-standing strains of religious fundamentalism and radicalism. The identities coalescing around these forms of religion, which also have well-known global origins, had already been locally constructed over decades and show great variation among Indonesia's provinces. For example, while the *Darul Islam* (the Abode of Islam) movements in Aceh, South Sulawesi, and West Java from the late 1940s to the mid-1960s were ideologically similar to the *Salafism* in the Middle East, these movements were rooted in local cultures, dealt with local problems, and showed different characteristics based on localities.

Increasingly, the rise of a network society in an information age—supported by the Internet and other media—has meant that the local (in this case, Indonesia) and the global have become more intensely and visibly connected. Through the technological power and growing use of the Internet as well as through the flow of money and people, Islamic radicalism in Indonesia has begun to develop links with similar radical Islamic movements in other parts of the world. This study details how these groups are using the Internet to disseminate the messages of Islamic radicalism, anti-Americanism, and other sentiments from local to global scales. The study pays specific attention to the role of the Internet as an identity tool for collective action that communicates the global citizenship of radical fundamentalists. In essence, the Internet has become a means of self-definition for Islamic fundamentalist movements worldwide (Beck 2000).

the Internet has become a means of self-definition for Islamic fundamentalist movements

Two cases are analyzed in the study. The first details the early wave of the *jihad* movement in Indonesia, which was marked by the formation of Laskar Jihad in the Maluku conflicts. The second case looks at the emergence of anti-U.S.-Israel sentiment in the aftermath of the 9/11 tragedy and subsequent events. Both cases investigate how Indonesian websites and e-mail lists were used to propagate a narrative of conspiracy involving the United States and Israel for the purposes of creating and disseminating a global *jihad.*[4] Based on these two cases, the monograph argues that, while the Internet presents a powerful new technological means of globally disseminating information, it must nevertheless be rooted in a local constellation of social forces and political power to be effective. The Internet facilitates the collapse of geographic barriers and the extremely fast creation of global meta-narratives. But these global narratives must ultimately be anchored in local contexts through resonance with local identities and local historical experiences.

In weaving together multiple insights, the study rests on the broader premise that understanding a set of phenomena such as the socio-political use of the Internet cannot be reduced to a single explanation from a single discipline. Instead, such analysis requires perspectives from disciplines across the social sciences and humanities. The ensuing sections use notions of identity politics, the concept of meta-narratives, and social theories of the Internet to detail how radical fundamentalist groups in Indonesia used the Internet.

Identity Politics and the Network Society

Creating identities is a universal human experience and fundamental source of meaning and social power. And *collective identity formation*—identities shared among individuals—is a primary driving force in contemporary world history (Castells 1997). These collective identities are the sources of resistance to globalization and the rise of network society, whose most salient forms today are information technologies, in particular the Internet (Lim 2003a). According to Castells (1997: 8), collective identities take three principal forms:

- *Legitimizing identities* created by dominant institutions of society—notably political regimes in control of the state apparatus and their followers—to extend and rationalize their rule;
- *Resistance identities* generated by those who are being devalued and/or stigmatized by the logic of domination; and
- *Project identities* that go beyond resistance and attempt to actively redefine positions in society (and, by so doing, to transform relations of power in the prevailing social structure).

Resistance identities play a critical role in fostering the rise of civil society against oppressive states and the hegemonic tendencies of global corporate capitalism. These identities become the moral fabric uniting people into communities of "collective resistance against otherwise unbearable oppression" (Castells 1997: 9). They can also further develop into projects that seek to change the course of history by using collective identities as a power base to (for example) overthrow existing regimes or create alternative communities at the margins of society and territorial spaces.

Although civil society often arises from resistance identities against the state, its sustenance ultimately requires the state's regulatory powers. In this sense, resistance or project identities must eventually transform themselves into the legitimizing identities of a new status quo. Such legitimizing identities bring together the "apparatuses" (such as political ideologies and religions) that are deeply rooted among people and that prolong the routines of state-civil society relations. However, as the Indonesian case will show, continued resistance could create identity projects that do not necessarily lead to a new period of national legitimation but instead threaten the vitality of civil society and the state.

Meta-narratives

Political language is designed to make lies sound truthful and murder respectable, and to give an appearance of solidity to pure wind (Orwell 1954: 177).

For societies in many modern nation-states, (re-)writing histories in an all-embracing and universal form is an instrumental tool for creating national identities from what were in many cases colonial territories composed of disparate peoples and societies. Such a storyline told of from "a" perspective, which thus precludes other perspectives, constitutes a *meta-narrative*.

"Meta" is defined here as "overall" or "totalizing." For Lyotard (1986), a "meta-narrative" is a big story, a story of mythic proportions that claims to account for, explain, and subordinate all lesser, little, local narratives. He rejects the totalizing claims of such a narrative. Foucault (1972) associates the concept of meta-narratives with legitimacy: While it can be used as a tool for social and political mobilization against perceived antagonistic, hegemonic forces, meta-narratives also seek to create their own hegemony. Meta-narratives reconstruct the past by providing a fixed framework with shared identity and filling it with a single collective memory. Through this process, they become very powerful, giving people a sense of solidarity and building their faith in social and cultural unity and ethnic or national values—all of which are the basis for collective action. A meta-narrative is an intentional awakening of people to their similarities and an assertion of homogeneity that is often intent on eradicating heterogeneity.

While a meta-narrative can be very useful—indeed, even necessary—in maintaining the unity, harmony, and solidarity of a nation-state, it leads mostly to inequality in power. Meta-narratives tend to identify certain bodies or groups—often the state, but also religious, racial, or cultural groups—as the rightful holders of power, thus legitimizing their right to dominate and marginalize others (Foucault 1972).

Meta-narratives constitute knowledge not through their correspondence with facts but by transmitting sets of rules that constitute social bonds. Meta-narratives are thus self-legitimating; they ratify themselves through their socially unifying function, which reifies a collective belief in them (Lyotard 1986). From the post-independence Sukarno regime to the Suharto regime, the Indonesian state apparatus was consciously used for decades to create meta-narratives that legitimized the state's power over people. People were fed these meta-narratives through the government's (particularly the President's) speeches, media propaganda, and reading materials taught in schools and enforced by the Ministry of Information, as well as police, and social regulations. This process has left Indonesia in a condition of *pre-modern knowledge*—that is, a knowledge largely based on narrative or story-like linear sequencing of events as told by the state and without alternative sources of verification or critical thought.

the Indonesian state apparatus was consciously used for decades to create meta-narratives

Suharto's regime ended in 1998, but the meta-narratives it and the Sukarno regime created have persisted in the minds of many Indonesians. At the same time, new and refurbished meta-narratives are being constructed both by factions of society vying for control over others and (according to some of these factional meta-narratives) by the state itself. Thus, while Indonesia's political reform has eroded the storyline of the country's authoritarian regimes, it has also opened a new era in the construction and struggle over new storylines.

The case studies presented below will show how different types of historiographies by nationalist and religious groups have created different histories or meta-narratives, grounded in selective remembering and selective forgetting. When a dominant power in the society—in this case the state—is changed or weakened in its level of power, such meta-narratives compete more boldly against each other. Some attack each other; some strengthen others. As this competition intensifies, what emerges is a polarization of groups that forge their own ideology and truth based on their own meta-narrative. The process results in continuing conflicts, some of which are violent and which generate spirals of continuing violence and revenge.

The Internet and Collective Action

Ideally, less dominant groups need media that (a) can avoid surveillance and censorship; (b) allow for one-to-one and many-to-many communications; and (c) are entrenched, broadly available, easy to use, and priced at a low or at least affordable cost (Lim 2003b). Such media also have features that make it inherently more difficult for a small number of people to control flows and content of information, knowledge, and ideological or symbolic representations. The Internet is now the most "convivial medium" that facilitates collective action (Lim 2003b). (The term "convivial medium" borrows from Ivan Illich's (1973) concept of "conviviality tools," which can be defined as tools or social arrangements that can enhance a person's freedom and autonomy.)

Freeman (1979) argues that one's means of communication is a key source of their entrance into collective action and social movement. The relatively cheap access and broad availability of the Internet can be considered a vital resource for the emergence of such actions and movements. However, we need to examine whether the Internet actually serves as such a resource, and which movements and organizations benefit from it. Internet use may benefit organizations or groups that have greater access to resources—including time and money, which they can invest into using the Internet. Mobilization through the Internet is thus more likely to be successful for collective action whose potential participants have access to the Internet (e.g., students rather than farmers). The Internet can also enable people to contribute resources (time, skills, or money) towards achieving collective goals. For example, an IT student can contribute his/her skills as well as money for the collective purpose of his/her group by using the Internet to do fundraising online.

Developing and practicing collective identity online may be more difficult for organizations or groups that mobilize around complex issues or causes. Organizations and groups committed to those issues or causes that society largely supports and that have already generated a high degree of societal trust and goodwill will more likely be able to develop online collective activism (Diani 2000: 397). Collective activism for less-visible causes often needs to generate such trust and collective identification, and thus requires more face-to-face interaction (Diani 2000: 397). Networks of organizations or groups that have already been established offline are also easier to establish online.

We also need to analyze how uses of the Internet can result in different means of communications and different ways to communicate— means and ways that may either prompt or inhibit mobilization. In this context, how does the Internet differ from other forms of mediated communication—i.e., the more traditional media?

Merlyna Lim

More traditional media have a one-way character of communication and a relatively clear distinction between producers and receivers of information. Such media make it is impossible for receivers to directly influence how, when, or what kind of information is received. The Internet, as Slevin (2000: 74) argues, blurs this dichotomy: Internet users can be both producers and receivers. Collective movements that use the Internet increase their potential of reaching audiences more directly. The Internet also provides a shorter time lag between events and the dissemination of information about those events than do more traditional media. And information distributed through the Internet also is relatively more difficult to censor than information distributed through more traditional media.

We should therefore expect these attributes to more easily facilitate identity formation, especially through "framing processes." (The term "frame" is borrowed from Goffman (1974) to denote the schemata of interpretations that enable people to locate, perceive, identify, and label occurrences within their life space and the society at large.) By rendering events or occurrences meaningful, frames function to organize experience and guide both personal and collective action.

However, several points call for special attention. For a movement's frame to be successful, it needs to resonate with the social mentalities of a culture and strike a chord in people's everyday experiences (Snow and Benford, 1988). The Internet does enable people in distant places to communicate directly and make their everyday experiences available to each other. Yet not all issues can easily be framed in cyberspace to resonate with such experiences.

Islamic Fundamentalism, Nationalism, and Collective Action in Cyberspace

Many observers argue that Islamic fundamentalism rejects nationalism. Indeed, they see Islamic fundamentalism's ideal—the establishment of a polity of believers (or *umma*)—as in conflict with the idea of the nation-state. For instance, Friedman (1994: 100) argues that fundamentalism's "shifting hegemony" provides alternative visions of the global situation that aim at the formation of a single world culture.

Many analysts also label Islamic fundamentalism as "postnational," a phenomenon that emerges as an alternative form for the organization of global traffic in resources, images, and ideas. The concept of "postnational" implies nation-states have become obsolete (Appadurai 1996). Indeed, fundamentalist figures themselves subscribe to this view. For example, Sayyid Qutb—an Egyptian fundamentalist leader—declares that a "Muslim's nationality is his [*sic*] religion" (Qutb quoted in Faksh 1997: 10).

However, as this study will show, Islamic fundamentalism has not always opposed the nation. At the same time, cyberspace does not make nation-states obsolete. This monograph illustrates how Islamic fundamentalism is not a matter of barring national difference, but rather of "constituting a discursive device which represents difference as…identity" (Hall 1992: 297). The case studies show that Islamic fundamentalist identity recognizes the national nature of conflicts but projects them beyond the nation. The common view of Islamic fundamentalism as essentially opposed to the

> *Islamic fundamentalism [and] cyberspace [do] not make nation-states obsolete*

nation-state (which it is said to regard as anti-Islam) is misleading. Rather, Islamic fundamentalism's fluid identity can take different forms according to the historical context, moving from nationalism to anti-nationalism to a mixture of both. The nation-state is still a basic unit of territorial power and popular identity; and Islamic fundamentalism sees seizing it and placing it under the aegis of Islam as a practical approach toward assembling building blocks for global Islamic hegemony.

This discourse about the global/national spatiality of Islamic fundamentalism identity resonates with similar discourse on cyberspace. Many have argued that the Internet is a medium of possibility in which individuals can go beyond the boundaries of their social selves (Turkle 1996; Hjarvard 2002). The Internet also blurs the boundaries between the spaces in which those who are connected exist (Freeman 1999). Cyberspace has created communities that are not necessarily physically or nationally bound, but which transcend the sacred boundaries of home and nation (Morley 1999).

However, these points do not imply that the Internet is detached from the realities of the social world. Rather, existing local and global power relations are extended into this new space instead of simply being displaced from the physical one. Connected to the corporality of its users, cyberspace is yet another zone in which conflicts are carried out. But while the existence and power relations of nation-states persist in cyberspace, cyberspace offers more flexible boundaries in which social identities can be amalgamated. An individual Internet user can choose to associate as a citizen of one nation-state, a global citizen of a Coca-Cola world, and as a member of Islamic *umma* or other groups without being restricted to any of these associations.

Through the mechanism of the Internet discussed above, all identities co-mingle and overlap. Such devices as meta-narratives, which explain and reconcile individuals as collectively part of a larger historical struggle, facilitate such melding. This phenomenon is illustrated by the of case of Laskar Jihad, which deftly combined Java-centered nationalism with Islamic fundamentalism to characterize discontent on the outer Indonesian island of Maluku as an anti-nationalist, anti-Islam, Judeo-Christian conspiracy.

Case Study I – Cyber-flow to Cyber-sword: Laskar Jihad Online

The Maluku Conflict and the Nationalist Meta-narrative

This conflict, which began in January 1999 and spread across the Maluku islands, a remote archipelago in the Eastern part of Indonesia, has taken the lives of at least 5,000 (and perhaps as many as 10,000) people of both faiths—Christianity and Islam. Nearly 700,000 have become refugees in sectarian violence (ICG 2000, 2002).

Maluku was a center of conflict 50 years earlier. During the war of Indonesian independence (1945–49), a group in this predominantly Christian province tried to declare Maluku's independence from the Republic of Indonesia, a predominantly Muslim state. Sukarno, the first president and proclaimed founding father of Indonesia, labeled this RMS separatist movement—"RMS" an acronym for the *Republik Maluku Selatan* (South Maluku Republic)—as "foreign colonialist" (Puar 1956: 3) or, more specifically, "the labor of Dutch reactionary element" (Puar 1956: 49). For Sukarno's regime, the issue of nationalism was paramount; in this light, it is understandable why the RMS was tagged as an important and dangerous anti-nationalist movement.[5] This characterization was also cultivated in formal history books used from elementary school upwards.[6] Thus, in the eyes of ordinary Indonesians on Java and other parts of the archipelago, Maluku has a dark history of disloyalty to the nation-state.

> *Maluku has a dark history of disloyalty to the nation-state*

In a country where Muslims make up about 88 percent of 235 million people—Christians comprise about 9 percent—Maluku is an anomaly, with roughly equal-sized populations of Muslims and Christians. However, most Indonesians believe that Maluku was initially predominantly Islam. The narrative of the state, propogated mostly through history class textbooks, also holds that Maluku inhabitants were once Muslims. It argues that this identity is demonstrated through the stories of the glory and prosperity of Ternate and Tidore Islamic Sultanates, before the Portuguese colonized these islands and forcefully converted their people to Christianity (Depdikbud 1976, 1977, 1983; Ohorella et al. 1993).[7] The official contemporary history of Maluku also finds parallels between the RMS and the Christian Ambonese—the ethnicity of local residents of Maluku—who were loyal to the island's Dutch colonizers. (The Dutch took over Maluku from the Portuguese in the 17th century.) The Christian Ambonese historically have been considered as unfaithful to the Indonesian state (Depdikbud 1983: 110). (Muslim Ambonese were described in this history as against the idea of RMS.) One officially sanctioned Indonesian history textbook labels the RMS as "an armed demolishment tactic of colonialism" (Depdikbud 1977: 90). Thus, in both Sukarno's and Suharto's narratives—which this study terms "nationalist meta-narratives" throughout—the RMS conflict was described as a horrible incident in Indonesian history and portrayed as an example of unfaithfulness by one ethnic group (the Ambonese) and one religion (Christianity) (Ohorella et al. 1993).

Five decades later, a minor quarrel between a Christian driver and a Muslim passenger precipitated the beginning of the contemporary, bloody, and enduring Maluku conflict, ending the relative harmony between the region's Christians and its Muslims. Enraged slaughter, savage mutilations, forced conversions, and the gratuitous destruction of property characterized the conflict following its outbreak in January 1999 (ICG 2000, 2002). Maluku's society since then has been formally (and forcefully) divided by religion—Christian versus Muslim—resulting in ongoing physical battles between the two. The battle between Christian "red" fighters and Muslim "white" fighters has continued to wipe out more lives. The discourse about the RMS has also re-emerged during this conflict, with the Indonesian nationalist meta-narrative identifying the RMS as a principal actor behind the conflict.

Laskar Jihad

Laskar Jihad was established on January 30, 2000 by its commander-in-chief, Ustadz Ja'far Umar Thalib, who proclaimed the existence of Laskar Jihad in front of more than 10,000 male Muslims gathered at Kridosono Stadium Yogyakarta. This paramilitary wing of the *Forum Komunikasi Ahlus Sunnah wal Jamaah* (FKAWJ, Communications Forum of the Followers of Sunnah) was formed in response to the government's inability to resolve the conflict in Ambon, the capital of Maluku province. It was meant to protect Ambon Muslims from a perceived Christian onslaught. In addition, according to some analysts, the group was also aimed at driving Indonesian President Abdurrahman Wahid from power (Hefner 2003). President Wahid, leader of the biggest moderate Muslim community in Indonesia, Nadhatul Ulama, had lost favor with some fundamentalist politicians mainly because of his closeness to Christians. His plan to initiate diplomatic relations with Israel also triggered resentment from some fundamentalist Islamic groups, including Laskar Jihad (Schulze 2002).

In April 2000, Laskar Jihad was introduced to the public when its members (along with other groups of Muslims) held a *Tabligh Akbar*[8] and a street demonstration in Jakarta calling for a *jihad* in the Maluku islands. Laskar Jihad arranged for military training to be given to volunteers at a camp in Bogor, near Jakarta. Despite President Wahid's objections, an estimated 3,000 *mujahedeen* departed for Ambon in the months after April 2000.

FKAWJ, the parent organization of Laskar Jihad, had been founded earlier in Solo by Ja'far Umar Thalib (a Madurese-Hadrami Arab) on February 14, 1998, only three months before the overthrow of President Suharto. Thalib was a central figure in the design of Laskar Jihad. The grandson of a Yemeni trader, Thalib has international experience, including fighting with the Afghan *mujahedeen* in 1988–89 and studying Islam in Lahore, Pakistan. Both experiences shaped his view of Islam as well as the struggle of Laskar Jihad in Maluku and other places in Indonesia. Long before the establishment of FKAWJ, Thalib had in 1993 already founded the *madrasah* (Islamic boarding school) *Ihya al-Sunnah Tadribud Du'at* in the village of Degolan, about 15 kilometers north of Yogyakarta. In this area, which contains a small mosque, several houses, and two cramped dormitories, the *salafy*[9] teaching of Thalib has been taught (Hefner 2003). With the founding of FKAWJ, Thalib's students at *Ihya al-Sunnah* were among Thalib's first followers and first Laskar Jihad fighters.

The core mission of the FKAWJ was to purify and spread Islam as expressed in the beliefs of the first generation of followers of the Prophet Muhammad. FKAWJ and the Laskar Jihad movement are considered "neo-fundamentalist" or neo-*Salafy* because they emphasized extreme political views not associated with earlier variants of *Salafism*, including those still popular in Saudi Arabia (Hasan 2001, Hefner 2003). One such extreme view is the firm belief that the United States and Israel, which neo-fundamentalists radicals term "Christians-Jews" or "Zionist-Crusaders," are leading a worldwide conspiracy to destroy Islam. Equally firm is the neo-fundamentalist view that Muslims must respond to this effort through armed *jihad* (Schulze 2002). This latter view (which this monograph terms global *jihad* meta-narrative) has been used by various *Salafy jihadis*[10] groups to justify their armed *jihad* actions.

Laskar Jihad claimed a three-part mission—social work, Muslim education, and what it terms a "security mission." It had over 10,000 members, 4,000 of whom were active in communal violence in the eastern part of Indonesia in Maluku and Poso.[11] Laskar Jihad also gained support from certain groups within the Indonesian National Army (TNI) and was able to embezzle money from these groups (Hefner 2003). Thalib claimed to have rejected approaches from Al-Qaeda, but Laskar Jihad supported the 9/11 attacks on the United States.

Three days after the Bali bombing on October 12, 2002, Laskar Jihad formally announced that it had disbanded, although the organization had already informally halted all activities one day before the Bali bombing. The reasons why the group disbanded—according to political analysts—were both practical and ideological, possibly came in response to orders from *Salafist* sheikhs in Yemen and Saudi Arabia. The leadership of Laskar Jihad had depended on religious guidance and sanction from these sheikhs throughout the conflict, and Thalib may have been pressured into dismantling the militia when the sheikhs began to claim conditions in the Maluku archipelago were no longer conducive for a justifiable *jihad*. Laskar Jihad was also accused by these *Salafist* sheiks as having deviated from *Salafi* principles by being too political and no longer simply devoted to "defending" Muslims. Finally, with the installment of Megawati Sukarnoputri as Indonesia's president in July 2001, the group may have been receiving less political and financial support from the Indonesian army (ICG 2001, 2002).

Laskar Jihad and the Media

In addition to its history, Laskar Jihad is of special interest for three other reasons related to the Internet and other information and communications technology (ICT), media discourse, and politics. First, Laskar Jihad was perhaps the most advanced Indonesian mass organization in using ICT. Second, Laskar Jihad utilized these new technologies in combination with more traditional media—print and electronic media—as well as with face-to-face communication. This combination of electronic communication with face-to-face mobilization extended Laskar Jihad's appeal well beyond what would have been possible using either mode alone. Lastly, the Laskar Jihad phenomenon is interesting because it illustrates the seamless amalgamation of ultramodern technology and traditional conservative ideology (Lim 2002).

From its beginning, FKAWJ incorporated ICT as one of its major organizational and operational tools—using fax machines and computers to organize and develop itself as well as to disseminate information. Later, the group used the Internet as a main tool to coordinate its operations and disseminate information as well as for fundraising and member recruitment in combination with traditional ways. FKAWJ also used print media—*Maluku Hari Ini* (The Maluku Today) daily newsletter; *Salafy* monthly; the weekly *Laskar Jihad Bulletin*; radio broadcasting; and some books published by FKAWJ or other publishers—to spread information regarding its ideology and activities, while at the same time remaining very dependent on face-to-face communications.[12]

Laskar Jihad's awareness of the benefits of media and ICT cannot be separated from the role of Ayip Syarifuddin, the architect behind Laskar Jihad. Syarifuddin stated that his weapons were the "sword and pen." He had worked as a journalist before joining Thalib in FKAWJ. For Syarifuddin, the media was an effective weapon for disseminating, socializing, defending, and fighting for an idea and an ideology. He believed that the existence of Islamic media is a significant force in balancing the domination of "Christian" (Western) media, which he argued had distorted the image of Islam (Hidayatullah 2002). His leadership of Laskar Jihad meant that Syarifuddin's view of the media's role—which was very much in line with the *jihad* ideology—became the underpinning for framing processes in all types of Laskar Jihad's media.

The formation of the FKAWJ coincided with the movement's increasing reliance on the Internet. Although commercial Internet access had been available since 1996 in some Indonesian university cities like Jakarta, Bandung, and Yogyakarta, it was only in late 1997 that commercial servers made the Internet broadly available in major cities on Java and Sumatra. Internet access was then extended to urban centers in Kalimantan, Sulawesi, and eastern Indonesia in late 1998. The FKAWJ leadership immediately recognized the potential of this new technology. The Internet allowed the core *Salafy* staff to maintain editorial and layout operations at the *Ihya al-Sunnah* school outside Yogyakarta while more than tripling its membership to include writers from around the country. And as Internet technology became more widely available throughout the country, the FKAWJ established branch offices in other cities and used the Internet and communications technologies to coordinate operations. Each branch office was equipped with an Internet connection and e-mail addresses, telephones, and fax machines.

Later, with the establishment of Laskar Jihad in January 2000, FKAWJ began to take full advantage of the Internet, as shown in the creation of the official website of Laskar Jihad (Laskar Jihad Online, at www.laskarjihad.or.id). The website subsequently became the major vehicle for developing and maintaining Laskar Jihad's presence and identity. Well-designed, bilingual (Indonesian and English), and regularly updated, Laskar Jihad Online showed how Laskar Jihad, while ultra conservative in its ideology, was ultramodern in its use of technologies and very much aware of the potential of the Internet and other ICT.

Laskar Jihad, while ultra conservative in its ideology, was ultramodern in its use of technologies

Beyond the website, Laskar Jihad also had a mailing list which kept members—who were scattered in 53 branch offices all over Indonesia—updated with the latest news about the Maluku conflict (Lim 2002).

Laskar Jihad Online

"*Remember! Death is already fixed; it won't be hastened by jihad, and will not be delayed by not carrying out jihad.*"

The above quotation appeared on Laskar Jihad Online, below the banner of Laskar Jihad on the website's homepage. In the left corner of the page appeared the blinking image of the symbol of Laskar Jihad—a pair of crossed sabers and the Qur'an (see Figure 1)—combined with the slogan of "*Jihad* in Ambon, fear nothing but (Allah)." This design and text com-

Figure 1. The Symbol of Laskar Jihad

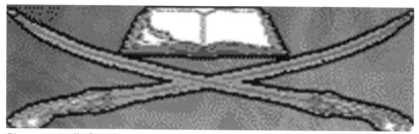

Picture originally from http://www.laskarjihad.or.id

bination concisely and efficiently disseminated the general message of this *jihad* group and labeled it as a religious project. (The image of crossed sabers and the Qur'an is commonly used by *jihadi* groups all over the world, including those in Saudi Arabia and Egypt.) Just as the logo and the banner indicated, Laskar Jihad Online was meant to incite Muslims to join the ranks of the *jihad* to fight against the Christians, particularly in Maluku and Poso, but also throughout Indonesia and beyond.

As noted earlier, Laskar Jihad Online (see Figure 2) was launched in June 2000 and was "officially" shut down by October 15, 2002. Web-mastered by Arif Rahman Hakim, a medical student of University of

Figure 2. Laskar Jihad Online Snapshot

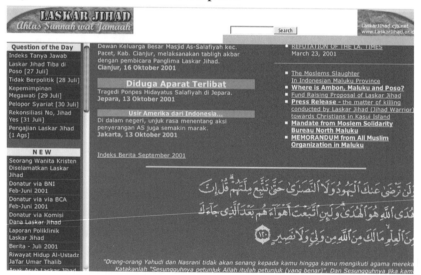

Picture originally from http://www.laskarjihad.or.id

Diponegoro Semarang, the website offered information about the ongoing conflicts in Indonesia in which Laskar Jihad was involved, with a focus on the Maluku conflict in textual, visual, and audio forms (Lim 2002).

Laskar Jihad Online published very comprehensive information about the FKAWJ and Laskar Jihad; it also attempted to put forth the basis and reasoning for the group's *jihad* actions. For instance, one of the website's sections dealt with the *fatwa* (authoritative treatises and jurisprudential issuances)—a crucial section in justifying Laskar Jihad's claim that its "call for *jihad*" to the Maluku fit under the rubric of defending Islam as a religion. The section consisted of translations of *fatwas* (from Arabic) that Laskar Jihad had received from the *Salafist* Sheiks in Saudi Arabia and Yemen. In these *fatwas*, the Saudi and Yemeni authorities appealed to all Muslims in Indonesia to carry out *jihad* in the name of God and defeat the "Christians who had attacked Muslims and occupied Muslim territory."

The importance of the imprimatur of Saudi and Yemeni authorities illustrates the global element in this local movement. By communicating these *fatwas* on the Internet, Laskar Jihad asserted a global identity while still paying attention to local issues. And using the Internet allowed Laskar Jihad to bypass local Islamic authorities—President Wahid, who was also a national Islamic leader, clearly ordered Laskar Jihad to stay away from Maluku—by presenting an "order" from "global" authorities.

Laskar Jihad asserted a global identity while still paying attention to local issues

Throughout the website, Laskar Jihad presented a carefully maintained image and representation. For example, in the "Question of the Day" section, Laskar Jihad attempted to show that it was inclusive, encompassing people from various places, strata, and classes by showcasing selected questions from around the globe as well as from a wide range of local people—from a teenager to a trishaw driver, from urban to remote. A section devoted to a "List of Adopted Children" attempted to show that the organization had a socially responsible and altruistic side.

The website's "Picture and Map" section was crucial to Laskar Jihad's aims. The section featured a map of Ambon showing territory captured by Laskar Jihad. It also included photo galleries of alleged Christian atrocities that contained mutilated bodies (which Laskar Jihad alleged were of

Muslim victims of massacres); burnt or damaged mosques; and graffiti on walls containing messages that insulted Islam (see Figure 3). All these photos were intended as graphic support for the organization's textual arguments in favor of *jihad*. Showing only dead Muslims and burnt mosques suggested that the Maluku conflict was a one-sided attack by Christians against Muslims rather than a violent struggle implicating both Christians and Muslims. The pictures are indeed very powerful, and draw on photography's implicit connotations of authenticity—connotations that presuppose images are an unmediated transcription of reality. These connotations make photographs very powerful in provoking emotions and disseminating a grievance to a larger collective of faithful adherents.

Figure 3. Example of Graffiti that Insults Islam

Picture originally from http://www.laskarjihad.or.id

During its first year of operation, Laskar Jihad Online featured stories and links to the websites of other *jihadi* groups around the world, including those in Chechnya, Palestine, Lebanon, Kashmir, and Afghanistan. This menu of places is typical for Islamic *jihad* online media. The *jihad* website of Hamas, Saudi Arabian-based *jihad* websites, and some of Bin Laden's propaganda video tapes (as shown on some *jihadi* websites) always include images of stories from Chechnya; Lebanon (the Israeli bombardment of the village of Qana); Palestine; Kashmir; Afghanistan; Indonesia; and (later) Iraq. These images are shown to justify the thesis that Christians (i.e., the West) and Jews are allied to destroy Islam. And, as with the graphic images posted on Laskar Jihad Online, the images available on other radical Islamic media are a very powerful generator of grievances and religious solidarity—especially among those who are "far away" from the geographic origin of the conflicts depicted. In one conversation in an Internet chat room, several Muslim teenagers who just visited the Indonesian version of Chechnya Jihadi websites said that they were as provoked and upset about atrocities allegedly perpetrated by a Christian-Jewish alliance against fellow Muslims in Chechnya as they were by the Maluku conflict. These teenagers stated that the Chechen photos gave them a full appreciation for *jihad* actions against the Christian-Jewish conspiracy all over the world, including in Maluku. One of them said: "As I saw the blood of my sisters and brothers, I burst in tears and drowned in a very deep sadness and unspeakable anger. We, Muslims, should do revenge. *Jihad* is the only answer."[13]

However, after 9/11, especially after the accusation of the U.S. administration that Laskar Jihad had ties to Al Qaeda, international links were quietly removed from Laskar Jihad Online. By removing these "virtual" links, Laskar Jihad also tried to detach itself from any "real" links to these organizations as claimed by Western media.

Beyond the website, Laskar Jihad had more than 1,400 members[14] on its Internet mailing list, which kept the group's troops, members, and supporters (scattered in 53 local agencies across Indonesia) updated with the latest news. Founded on May 17, 2000, the mailing list used Yahoo! as its platform and was written in Indonesian. Some of the news posted to this mailing list was directly derived from the website of Laskar Jihad, while the rest was claimed to have been posted directly from Maluku. The mailing list was not meant to provide a space for dialogue: Only moderators were allowed to post. It was actually a one-directional newsletter that provided what it called news "from the battlefield." This mechanism shows how the digital setting of cyberspace allows a certain group of people—in this case, the moderators of the mailing list—to filter what it disseminates and thus attempt to restrict what its audiences read.

Many of the messages disseminated by the mailing list were written as personal journals. By framing the conflict personally, Laskar Jihad Online defined the putative conflict between the West and Islam through the feelings, attitudes, and voices of individuals—making its message more appealing to target audiences. Through its website and mailing list, Laskar Jihad married a communal resistance based on religiosity with the postmodern weapon of information technology (Lim 2002). This combination was exemplified by the Laskar Jihad Online webmaster Arif Rahman Hakim—a medical student by day and a cyberspace holy warrior by night—who wrote in a mission statement that his intention was "to show the software site of *jihad*, a holy war" (Ebiz Asia 2001).

Fusion of Nationalist and Global Jihad Meta-narratives
Laskar Jihad's main justification for its *jihad* war in Maluku was taken primarily from the thesis of Rustam Kastor, a retired Ambonese brigadier who is arguably the group's ideological father. Kastor elaborated the thesis in his three books. The first—*Fact, Data, and Analysis of RMS-Christian Political Conspiracy in Destroying Muslims in Ambon-the Maluku*—was published in early 2000 (well before April 2000, when the actual *jihad* war started in Ambon) and became a bestseller in Indonesia.

In his books, Kastor provided a historical justification for sending Laskar Jihad to the Maluku. According to this justification, the Dutch-supported Christians in Maluku were planning to re-establish the Republic of the South Maluku (RMS) and to wipe out the Muslims there. In Kastor's opinion, the Protestant Church of the Maluku (*Gereja Protestan Maluku*, or GPM) was not the only force behind the conflict, but had been joined by the branch association of the "Christian-Nationalist"[15] of the Indonesian Democratic Party in Struggle (*Partai Demokrasi Indonesia Perjuangan*, PDI-P), the party of the Indonesian president Megawati Sukarnoputri. Moreover, according to Kastor, the conflict was a part of Christianization project going on throughout Indonesia, which ultimately supports the Christian-Jewish international project in destroying Islam worldwide. Kastor's books were available online for free downloading (Kastor 2000); the links were accessible from Laskar Jihad Online.

To support this thesis, Laskar Jihad Online reiterated a line included in all state-sanctioned history books—namely, that the Maluku once were Islamic islands before Western colonizers forcefully converted them to Christianity. Laskar Jihad claimed to represent Islam itself; it claimed a holy duty to purify the Muslims in Indonesia and lead them back to the right path, avoiding entrapment by the tricks and domination of non-Muslims, and this could only be fulfilled by the application of the Muslim law (Islamic *sha'ria*) throughout Indonesia.

> Listen to me, supporters of Americans. Listen to me, supporters of
> the World Church Council. Listen to me supporters of the Zionist-
> Crusaders. Listen to me Jews and Christians, we, Muslims, invite
> the U.S. troops to prove their power here in Maluku. Let's fight fer-

vently. Let's prove that for the umpteenth time Muslims cannot be subjugated by their over-exaggerated physical power. The second Afghan war will happen in the Maluku if you are determined to threaten us, hey Americans. Now, hey you Americans, you have suffered losses in various huge attacks in Afghanistan. Let us bravely meet in the battlefield (Thalib; aired by SPMM[16] radio on May 1, 2, and 3, 2002; cited in Munindo 2000, translated from the Indonesian).

As shown in above quotation, Laskar Jihad was fond of linking the Maluku conflict with the United States (FKAWJ 2002). In fact, Laskar Jihad used the words "Jews," "Christians," "Crusader," "Zionist," and "Americans" interchangeably, as if they all represented one person or one group of people or one identity group. Such conflations were found again and again in Laskar Jihad Online, in the Laskar Jihad mailing list, in Laskar Jihad's print publications, and in the books and speeches of Laskar Jihad leaders.

Laskar Jihad also equated Christians in Maluku with RMS and even created a new term for RMS: *Republik Maluku Serani* (Republic of Christian Maluku). The term implicitly accused all Christians on Maluku of participating in the struggle for sovereignty and separation from the Indonesian state. And when a Christian Ambonese medical doctor named Alex Manuputty established the Maluku Sovereignty Forum (*Front Kedaulatan Maluku*, FKM) at the end of 2000 and suggested its ideological connection to the RMS movement in the 1950s, the move seemed to fulfill Laskar Jihad's Christian conspiracy thesis (Bräuchler 2003). Since then, this "conspiracy" has been used by Laskar Jihad as its pretext to attack Christians.

With its stories from the battlefield supported by graphic pictures of victims, Laskar Jihad also tried to reconstruct all of Islam as the victim. For example, Laskar Jihad accused the Indonesian government (namely, the military) of taking the side of Christians in Maluku, and also

"We do jihad for the country, nation-state, and God (Islam)."

used Maluku as evidence that Indonesia has always marginalized Islam. This narrative asserted that the country's Christian minority had stirred up the state to victimize Indonesian Muslims, mirroring the Islamic fundamentalist narrative that all Christians victimize Muslims worldwide. In this context, the putative resurgence of RMS spelled separatism—an unforgivable sin to Indonesian nationalists—and became an unfalsifiable justification for attacking Christians in Maluku. Maluku's past connections to the Dutch as well as the present connections of the GPM in Ambon Maluku to the GPM in the Netherlands also legitimized the Christianization issue for Laskar Jihad's followers. Fusing nationalism with Global *Jihad* meta-narratives gave a powerful synergy to Laskar Jihad's case for intervention. As the group's leader Thalib always said, "We do *jihad* for the country, nation-state, and God (Islam)."

Laskar Jihad and Cyber-community

Beyond its website and mailing list, Laskar Jihad rapidly disseminated its meta-narratives throughout many other Islamic websites, regardless of whether they were linked to Laskar Jihad Online. The webmaster of Laskar Jihad Online was persistent enough to keep sending an announcement about the website to many guest-books, mailing lists, and chat rooms. Almost all common website shortcuts related to Ambon[17] were owned by Islamic partisans in the Maluku struggle. The reaction of cyber-Muslims towards the Maluku conflict was notably more intense than that of cyber-Christians.[18]

Laskar Jihad also extended its message through online media. Online newspapers such as Marsinah.com, Hidayatullah.com, and Republika.co.id were dependent on Laskar Jihad Online as their source for news on the Maluku conflict. Many times, these online newspapers just published Laskar Jihad articles without any modification or investigation.

As soon as Laskar Jihad went online in June 2000, many other websites sprung up that were devoted to Muslims in Maluku and elsewhere in Indonesia. These websites had hyperlinks to Laskar Jihad Online.[19] In addition, some existing global and Indonesian websites (both Islamic and secular) began to devote sections or pages to the Maluku *jihad* as well. Some of the official websites of Indonesian universities and schools also linked to Laskar Jihad Online, as did personal Muslim websites. In fact, some Muslim youth transformed the term *jihad* into "cyber-*jihad*." These youth assumed that the world was dominated by Western-based media biased against Islam; they felt that only the Internet provided a free space for Muslims to engage in their struggle. Their logic dictated that Muslims should fight by creating as many Islamic (*jihad*) websites as possible.

Although not directly influenced by the example of Laskar Jihad Online, other Islamic radicalism websites—both those who claim to be *Salafist* and non-*Salafist*—emerged on the Internet between 2000 and 2002. Among these were the websites of Majelis Mujahidin Indonesia; Hizbut Tahrir Indonesia, the Defender of Islam Front; Hamas Indonesia; and fundamentalist news websites such as Suara Muslim and IslamOnline. All of these websites subscribed to the meta-narratives of Laskar Jihad, and they would refer to the Laskar Jihad Online articles when they discussed the Maluku conflict.

Net to Street: Linkages to Other Print Media and Physical Space
Laskar Jihad Online's reach also extended beyond the Internet. Some print media outlets also turned to the site first to get their news and information about the Maluku conflict. These print media—such as *Republika* newspaper, *Suara Hidayatullah, Media Dakwah,* and *Sabili*—used Laskar Jihad Online's images and discourse in their own reports. They thus lent credence to Laskar Jihad's meta-narratives instead of providing their own accounts of the conflict.

These media outlets reported the ongoing conflict in Maluku with sensational stories and provocative headlines that claimed the conflict was a pilot project of the Christianization project in Indonesia and a part of a Jewish and Christian plan to cleanse the world of Muslims. *Sabili*, for example, ran news stories with headlines such as "Moslim Cleansing: Ambon is not alone" (Sabili 1999a); "Christianization: Volume 2" (Sabili 1999b); and "Thousands of Muslims were Slaughtered by the Infidel Christians" (Sabili 2000). Following Sabili's path, the *Suara Hidayatullah* also tried to popularize the Zionist-Crusader conspiracy theory by making headlines such as "Uncover the Practice of the GGG: Gold-Gospel-Glory, The Moslem Cleansing in Ambon" (Suara Hidayatullah 1999). Under its article entitled "The *Jihad* War is Continuing in Ambon" (Media Dakwah 1999: 42–44), the *Media Dakwah* not only referred to the "Zionist-Crusader" conspiracy, but also equated the Maluku conflict to a Christian crusade and called on Indonesian Muslims to join the *jihad.*

Before the emergence of Laskar Jihad Online, these media outlets had made no explicit link between the *jihad* action and nationalism. *Jihad* was formerly seen as a purely religious action to be done by Muslims for other Muslims—in the name of God. But after the launch of Laskar Jihad

Online, these Islamist media heavily reflected the Laskar Jihad's fusion of Global *Jihad* meta-narrative and nationalist meta-narrative.

Furthermore, with the emergence of Laskar Jihad Online, these media outlets brought a sense of immediacy about the conflict to their readers with personalized "stories from the battlefield." Images and personal stories of Laskar Jihad fighters and supporters in Ambon and other areas in the Maluku islands brought narratives vividly alive and thus were more convincing and influential than standard news reports.

The case of the *Republika* newspaper shows the distinct influence of Laskar Jihad Online. Before the launch of the website, *Republika*—unlike mainstream newspapers who were dependent on a military news office as their source—was highly dependent on its understaffed group of field reporters. *Republika* therefore did not publish many articles about the conflict, apparently because it didn't have enough staffers to write them. Also, while this newspaper was biased towards Muslims (and against Christians), it still tried to be uncontroversial and show balanced views.[20] However, after the emergence of Laskar Jihad Online, *Republika* began frequent coverage of Maluku. The newspaper had become very dependent on the website of Laskar Jihad and even used it as the main source of information about the conflict. As a result, *Republika* ended up publishing highly biased reports that reflected the views and ideology of Laskar Jihad.

In addition to these newspapers and magazines, books about Maluku published by Islamic writers/organizations between 2000 and 2002 also frequently referred to Laskar Jihad Online.[21] Many of the storylines, arguments, and even photographs in these books were derived directly from Laskar Jihad Online.

However, none of these linkages were more obvious or effective than the linkages Laskar Jihad itself initiated. The Laskar Jihad leadership demonstrated great skill in linking its Internet resources to other communications media. They used the Internet to send daily reports on the Maluku conflict to each of Laskar Jihad's branch offices around the country. Each office downloaded the messages, which were already laid out in a desktop publishing format. The files were printed out on a single, two-sided sheet of paper to create the newsletter *Maluku Today* (*Maluku Hari Ini*). The left of the publication's letterhead featured Laskar Jihad's logo with its open Qur'an set above two crossed swords. On the bottom of the back page appeared information on Laskar Jihad's website, e-mail address, information for prospective donors, and local branch address. At the height of the group's operations, in July 2000 and April 2001, Laskar Jihad officials in branch offices made thousands of copies of *Maluku Today*, which were distributed to the public by young male volunteers. Clad in the *jihadi's* trademark tunic, trousers, and turban, these volunteer hawkers positioned themselves at traffic lights in cities across Indonesia. They distributed the newsletter for free but with the understanding—which they conveyed in none-too-subtle fashion by passing a bucket in front of car windows—that donations to the Maluku campaign were welcome.

Laskar Jihad...demonstrated great skill in linking its Internet resources to other communications media

Laskar Jihad also operated a monthly *Salafy* tabloid and the bi-weekly national bulletin of Laskar Jihad (*Buletin Laskar Jihad Ahlus Sunnah wal Jama'ah*), both of which were more sophisticated than the daily newsletter. The bulletin was a 16-page bi-weekly featuring articles (mainly about Laskar Jihad's activities and FKAWJ's ideology) with color photos and some advertisements. Once again, the publications used photographs of Muslim victims and destroyed mosques to lend verisimilitude to stories about the Christian atrocities against Muslims. Some articles in this bi-weekly bulletin were derived from the content of Laskar Jihad Online. Laskar Jihad Online also promoted the bulletin through a pop-up window on its index page. Sold for less than $1 and sometimes even given away, the circulation of *Maluku Today* was about 100,000.[22]

The *Salafy* tabloid was actually launched long before the establishment of FKAWJ. A year after the founding of the *Ihya al-Sunnah* school of Ja'far Umar Thalib, several of Thalib's students got together to create *Salafy*, a glossy-covered yet inexpensive monthly dedicated to militant *Salafism* teaching *a la* Thalib. Using desktop publishing technologies, the staff of *Salafy* did most of the editorial and layout work at their homes or at the *Ihya al-Sunnah* school. Printing was then out-sourced to a shop in the nearby town of Klaten. *Salafy* became the official organ of the FKAWJ after that organization was established in February 1998. These tabloids and bulletins were sold across Indonesia through the branch offices of Laskar Jihad, mosques, street vendors, kiosks, and small shops. But while both publications operated outside cyberspace, they were in fact mostly print versions of Laskar Jihad Online after the website's launch.

Besides passing a bucket during traffic lights and fundraising through its website, Laskar Jihad also used donation boxes in restaurants, cafes, and food stalls to raise money, especially in Padang restaurants and kiosks (*rumah makan* and *warung Padang*). Humble in appearance, this fundraising method was effective; it could sometimes pull money from those who did not actually plan to give. With such a grass-roots style of outreach and information distribution, it is not surprising that Laskar Jihad could gain popularity and funding, especially in urban areas. But what is remarkable about Laskar Jihad's message is that it reached not only Indonesia's lower classes—an appeal in line with the classic assumption that poverty and lack of knowledge are the basis of radicalism—but also penetrated the country's knowledge centers and top universities, such as the Bandung Institute of Technology (ITB) and University of Gajah Mada (UGM). The printed version of Laskar Jihad Online and/or *Maluku Today* could be found on the announcement boards of student associations in ITB and in a small *madrasah* in Solo.

The proliferation and dissemination of Laskar Jihad's messages demonstrates that the organization knew how to use the Internet (and other advanced media and communication tools), cyber-networks, and other types of networks extremely well to disseminate its vision for an Islamic society. By fusing the nationalist and Global *Jihad* meta-narrative, Laskar Jihad gained power and even tacit legitimation from some elements of the state and society. In fact, Indonesian Vice President Hamzah Haz (who served under Megawati) openly supported Laskar Jihad and even opened the first National Congress of FKAWJ in May 2002 (Tempo 2002).

Jihad, the Weapon of the Weak

Laskar Jihad Online sought to inspire and mobilize people. The website was not a careful intellectual presentation of an ideological program or theological position. It did, however, have its place in a significant modern tradition of thought and faith in the Muslim world. The so-called "fundamentalists" seldom advocate a return to medieval conditions of life and often reject medieval scholastic formulations as strongly as they reject contemporary secularist ideologies. Most Muslims within this tradition do not advocate violence as a response to contemporary problems. However, some recognize that coercive power is a decisive aspect of the contemporary Muslim world. Laskar Jihad's website and mailing list both detailed a long list of narratives in which Muslims have been defeated and oppressed by superior (Christians and Jews) military force, arguing further that force can only be countered by force. The website sought to mobilize the weak and the powerless by offering a way to take hold of the sources of power.

The simplicity and clarity of Laskar Jihad's argument is the strength of the organization. The form of the argument's syllogism is familiar to every high school debater:

(a) *Describe the problem* (many Muslims in the Maluku have been killed);

(b) *Explain the causes of the problem* (Christian separatist groups killed these Muslims as part of an international Zionist-Christian crusade against Islam); and

(c) *Propose a clear solution to the problem that addresses the causes you have described* (the holy war, *Jihad!*).

The logical simplicity of the argument forecloses any need to understand Islamic theology, specific political grievances in different lands, or the structure and organization of the group summoning you to war. By presenting a black-and-white picture and identifying an unambiguous enemy, Laskar Jihad was successful in promoting a resistance identity and even turning it into a project identity (Castells 1997).

While Laskar Jihad's project itself, according to some political analysts, was only domestic and political (Hefner 2003), the project's tone and impact go beyond these purposes. However, Laskar Jihad was not successful in inciting people to join its version of the *jihad*. While Laskar Jihad's media propaganda helped a large number of Indonesian Muslims to understand and appreciate the group's *jihad* action, most of these Indonesians did not go to the battlefield to fight, and most Muslims interviewed claimed that they

Laskar Jihad was not successful in inciting people to join its version of the jihad

would not do so.[23] Yet none of 16 Muslims interviewed for this research categorically said that Laskar Jihad had been wrong. Indeed, most of those interviewed said that, although they had not fully agreed with all of Laskar Jihad's activities, the group's *jihad* action had been reasonable and understandable. Seven out of the 16 said that *jihad* action had been the only way out for Muslims in Maluku because the government could not handle the situation and Christians were heavily supported by international links. Twelve people believed that the conflict had been religious in nature and initiated by the Christian separatist movement of RMS; three others, while believing that the RMS had been behind the conflict, were not sure whether the conflict was religious or purely political. While only four firmly believed that the RMS must have been a part of global conspiracy against Islam, nine others thought that the possibility of international (Western-Christian) links to the conflict should not be overlooked. However, each of these nine people refused to consider the involvement of Israel. None of these Muslims interviewed actually condemned the physical violence of Laskar Jihad, but all but two did express dislike for it; the exceptions were two female Muslims who persistently expressed that the conflict was purely political and that both parties—Laskar Jihad and RMS—should have been condemned.

These interviewees' voices cannot be generalized as the voices of Indonesians as a whole; nor are they methodologically representative of a majority of the country's population. However, the result of these interviews portrays the dilemma that Indonesian Muslims faced over the Maluku conflict. After all, in the minds of most Indonesians (particularly those on Java, where more than three-fifths of the national population lives), RMS has always been considered inimical to Indonesia's national integrity—especially in light of how nationalism has been cultivated in official meta-narratives. The concept of one *ummah*—i.e., that Muslims belong to the Muslim community worldwide and thus should defend any Muslim anywhere in the world who is hurt by a non-Muslim—also fed into the conceptual dilemma over the Maluku conflict. Combined with a belief in Global *Jihad* meta-narratives, *ummah* made it difficult for a Muslim to condemn Laskar Jihad for its exhortations to violently defend a nation and Islam in the Maluku. And for a moderate Muslim who does not necessarily support *jihad*, Laskar Jihad's actions have a certain resonance with either or both their religious and national identities. These factors make it clear why the broader Muslim population did not consistently condemn Laskar Jihad's actions and stance toward the conflict.

Case Study II – Indonesia and the Global Jihad Meta-narrative: "Scaling Up While Scaling Down"

While the previous section focuses more on the case of domestic conflict, this section looks at the creation and dissemination of conspiracy theories that strengthen the Global *Jihad* meta-narratives in cyberspace—meta-narratives used to justify the wave of Islam radicalism in the aftermath of 9/11. The section extends the discussion from the previous section by documenting how these conspiracy theories provoked people with no actual experience in religious oppression or conflict into virtually generating examples of such oppression or conflict at local levels. These people then fed these "new" episodes into global narratives—by using all the tools of the Internet and other ICT to generate news (invent, create, and embellish it); give it identity markers (oppression of Islam); and simplify it into news slugs and graphic representations that created or played into meta-narratives.

Political mailing lists in Indonesian cyberspace range from nationalist to religious. This case study, however, focuses on the nation's Islamic mailing lists, particularly fundamentalist and radical ones. These mailing lists do not represent all of Indonesia's political cyber-communities, or even all its Islamic cyber-communities. Islam Liberal and KMNU2000 (a youth organization of the moderate Islamic organization *Nahdlatul Ulama*) are examples of moderate Indonesian cyber-mailing lists.

"Islam Under Attack": The Radical Dualism Frame of 9/11

On the morning after 9/11, President George W. Bush gave a speech in which he said the following:

> The deliberate and deadly attacks which were carried out yesterday
> against our country were more than acts of terror, they were acts of
> *war*. This will require our country to unite in steadfast determination
> and resolve. *Freedom* and *democracy* are under attack.... This will be
> a monumental struggle of *good* versus *evil*, but good will prevail.
> (Bush 2001, emphasis added)

These remarks are just a few of the many remarks with which Bush attempted to characterize 9/11 as an act of war in simple, emotional, and Manichean terms. Repeatedly using the terms "good" and "evil" and naming the post-9/11 policy a "war" on terrorism was an effective political choice. These rhetorical moves helped to unite the country behind the Bush administration's interpretation and response to the attacks and to exclude other interpretations and understandings.

In the months following the attacks, U.S. media networks used images and discourses to frame 9/11 within the narrative Bush had created. The result was a war frenzy that failed to provide a coherent account of what happened, why it happened, and what would count as reasonable U.S. responses. The dominant discourses, frames, and representations that informed the media and public debate show how the mainstream media in the U.S. privileged the "clash of civilizations" model (Huntington 1993) and strengthened a binary dualism between Islamic terrorism and Western civilization. In essence, these media circulated pro-war agitation and discourses that called for some form of military intervention. While some media channels did not position Islam in opposition to the West, these more moderate channels still encouraged simplification of the situation by expressing the binary dualism of Islamic terrorism versus civilization.

For Muslim societies, perhaps the single most disturbing image used during this rhetorical campaign was Bush's use of the word "crusade." This word, historically rooted in the context of religious war between Christianity and Islam, is always open to religious interpretation. And by using "crusade" in the context of the war between "good" and "evil," between "us" and "them," the Bush administration's campaign became readable as "Christian" to Muslims. The campaign secured its own positive identity through the stigmatization of Osama bin Laden and other terrorists. In so doing, however, it opened a door for the "othering" of Muslims all over the world, including Indonesian Muslims.

As the Bush administration continues to claim to be "the right" ("the good," "us"), the danger multiplies—not only for the Islamic Other ("them") who may be subjected to violence, but for the Western "us" that are at constant risk of being de-legitimized. Gaining legitimacy through "othering" has an inherent fragility: It must constantly be fed by the illusory inferiority (moral or otherwise) of the Other. And those who are "othered" tend to fight against their marginalization and to be trapped in the same pattern of radical dualism—"othering" those who have "othered" them. This process is exactly what has happened between the West and Muslims. These mindsets serve only to foment more antagonism and aggression—emotions that have as their end total victory.

Resistance Identity and Contesting Radical Dualism

As noted in earlier sections, the resurgence of Islamic radical fundamentalism in Indonesia began before 9/11. Laskar Jihad and other *jihadi* groups became active long before 9/11, and some radical fundamentalist groups also existed in cyberspace before those events. With or without

9/11, the radical fundamentalist groups that had stepped into the Indonesian political arena since the overthrow of Suharto would have kept trying to disseminate their ideology and influence more people to join them by using any kind of media, including the Internet.

However, the Bush administration's radical dualism pitting terrorism against the West certainly triggered more resistance among Indonesia's Muslims—not only among radicals but also moderates. The combination of this radical dualism and a prevalent pre-disposition among Muslims against the so-called "Zionist-Crusaders" (the United States and Israel) pushed a large number of Indonesian Muslims to respond intensely to the aftermath of the 9/11 attacks and to bond through a feeling of victimization.

In Indonesian cyberspace, a remarkable reaction occurred towards the 9/11 attacks. Discussions on the tragedy began almost immediately. At first, there was a great deal of sympathy toward Americans. But resentment very quickly replaced this sympathy as some cyber-community members became antagonized by the Bush administration's actions. New mailing lists devoted exclusively to discussing bin Laden and the *jihad* movement were set up in the first few days after 9/11. Postings related to the tragedy appeared most frequently in religion-based mailing lists and websites, particularly Islamic ones (Lim 2004). The news offered on these mailing lists originated mainly from other mailing lists and websites (most of which were global mailing lists and mailing lists of Indonesian communities abroad) or from the translations or transcriptions of other forms of media (newspapers, books, television, and radio). Unsurprisingly, the earliest postings about 9/11 in many Islamic forums directly jumped to the issue of Islam and terrorism instead of narratives of the event itself.

An example of these discussions comes from the mailing list of a Bandung-based moderate Islamic group. The first 9/11-related posting appeared in this mailing list less than 12 hours after the attack: a religious-sounding poem that described the unreality of the event and the unfairness of the West's reaction—viewed by the author as slander—on Muslim society:

> If I see the real painting of today's event
> I could not say it was a Hollywood movie
> Because the real tears were there
> If I read again the real news of today's event
> I could not say it was a Hollywood movie

Because the real vengeance was there
If I see again the today's event
I could not say it was a Hollywood movie
Because the real slander was there (translated from Indonesian).[24]

Many of the 9/11-related postings on this mailing list followed in this vein. Postings in the following weeks about 9/11 were all rooted in the belief that Israel had perpetrated the attacks while the United States blamed the Arab world. In two subsequent days, one poster sent 23 e-mails, 20 of which asserted that Israel indeed was the actor behind the tragedy. The mailing list was full of e-mails with subject lines such as "Anti-U.S. and Jews, the Brain of WTC Tragedy," "Americans and Zionist are united to fight Islam," "4,000 Israeli[s] absent on the day of WTC attack," and "Israel is the puppet master of WTC tragedy." All were written in Indonesian, which implies how quickly the anti-U.S. line was translated in cyberspace. Some of these forwarded e-mails originated from the Association of Indonesian Muslim Intellectuals in New York (Lim 2004).

Other Islamic mailing lists, especially the Islamist/*Salafist* ones,[25] shared this tendency to blame Israel and accuse the United States of slander. E-mails with subject lines such as "4,000 Israeli[s] absent on the day of WTC attack" (which sometimes appeared with a different subject line, such as "4,000 Jews did not report to work on 9–11–01") and "Americans and Zionist are united to fight Islam" (which sometimes appeared with the subject line "CIA and Mossad's Complicity in 9–11 attacks") appeared in a multitude of other mailing lists. One other very popular related e-mail was titled "CNN used 1991 footage of Palestinians celebrating 9–11" and accused CNN of using a video of Palestinians cheering the death and destruction of 9/11 that was actually 10 years old. An e-mail in which CNN officially denied the claim and which contained a retraction from the author of the original e-mail (who now said that his information was wrong and that he no longer believed the story) was never widely circulated.

By a couple of weeks after the event, the information spreading through Indonesian mailing lists and other Internet pages had totally shifted from the event itself to positive discussions about Osama bin Laden, Israel as the possible 9/11 perpetrator, negative opinions about Israel, and the importance of *jihad*. The leader of Laskar Jihad stated that the attack on the WTC and the Pentagon was the response of God—*Allah*

Subhanahu wa Ta'ala—to the arrogance of the United States (Thalib 2001a). In an article entitled "Die America," he pronounced:

> We wish you to mourn well, the United States of America. Hopefully
> you are learning something from your stupid arrogance. To Muslims
> we ask you to be happy as the revenge for all humiliations and ter-
> ror(ism) against all Muslim countries committed by the greatest ter-
> rorist in the world has already been taken (Thalib 2001b: 10, trans-
> lated from Indonesian).

Most discussants positioned Osama bin Laden as a scapegoat or even a victim of a conspiracy by Israel in order to discredit Islam. In some ways,
Islamic fundamentalism groups in Indonesia positioned bin Laden as a
hero; yet they also did not want to be suspected of having links with him.[26]

Before the United States invaded Afghanistan, Indonesian cyberspace
still contained some voices that showed sympathy towards Americans—
especially on the KMNU2000 mailing list. However, the U.S. war to top-
ple the Taliban in Afghanistan triggered in both radical and moderate
mailing lists the circulation of fundamentalist narratives about a U.S. conspiracy to destroy Islam. In the eyes of many participating in these lists,
the United States was no longer a victim of terrorism but had become a
terrorist. After the launch of the Afghanistan invasion in October 2001,
many articles from fundamentalist mailing lists circulated in Indonesian
cyberspace; these articles tried to link the United States, terrorism, and
Zionism, and portrayed the 9/11 attack as an attempt by the United States
and Israel to justify the war against Islam (Primamorista 2001).

At this point, Indonesian online media as well as mailing lists and websites had become caught up in the rhetoric of Osama bin Laden and the Taliban, which stated that the United States was not fighting against only them but against Muslims all over the world. The line of these media mirrored the logic of President Bush: His statement that "Either you are with us, or you are with the terrorists" was transformed into "not supporting Taliban and bin Laden equals supporting Bush." And even neutral opinions expressed in Indonesian cyberspace about the Taliban and bin Laden were

even neutral opinions expressed...about the Taliban and bin Laden were now interpreted as supporting the United States

now interpreted as supporting the United States and attacking Islam. To avoid being accused as betraying Islam, cyberspace participants played it safe by demonstrating hatred (otherwise known as "writing hatred") for the United States.[27] Consequently, information spread in Indonesian cyberspace in the wake of the U.S. attack on Afghanistan inclined to be positive about Taliban and bin Laden and negative about the United States. Pro-Taliban online sources such as Afghan Online, IslamOnline, and Al-Jazeera.com became major references of information in Indonesian cyberspace.

Addicted to Conspiracy Theories

Some cyber-activists in Indonesia who assumed that Western media were biased against Islam suggested initiating a cyber-*jihad* against the United States. These cyber-activists wrote, translated, forwarded, and disseminated only anti-U.S. information, assuming that pro-U.S. information could already be easily obtained from Western media. However, a majority of Indonesian Internet users are not active users of the medium; they read information that comes to their mailboxes rather than actively searching for information. Based on observations of some Indonesian mailing lists, the country's active Internet users are not numerous but are extremely active online and inclined to forward information to all mailing lists of which they are members. These *superactive* Internet users also diligently translate information from other languages (mostly English) and sometimes compile information from various sources and forward them in one message. Superactive Internet users are mostly male, information-technology savvy, highly educated, and have physical science or engineering educational backgrounds. While not many superactive Indonesian users seem addicted to conspiracy theories, those users who fit this characterization have filled up the traffic of Indonesian cyberspace with various conspiracy narratives pitting the United States and Israel (or Christians and Jews) against Islam.

Subsequent events such as the Bali bombing in October 2002, the war between the United States and Iraq (which began with the U.S. attack in March 2003), and the Jakarta Marriott bombing in August 2003 all brought out more stories on conspiracy theory. Not surprisingly, all these stories are also framed by an overriding sentiment against the United States and Israel. The most popular theory about the Bali blast was propagated by Ustadz Abu Bakar Ba'asyir, a leader of Majelis Mujahiddin Indonesia

(MMI) suspected of being linked with the *Jemaah Islamiyah*. He stated that the bombing must have been the work of American CIA agents because only Americans have the capability to put such a bomb together. Leaders of the Justice Party (*Partai Keadilan*), Hizbut Tahrir, the Defender of Islam Front, and some legislators from President Megawati Sukarnoputri's political party supported this view (Eriyanto and Harsono 2001).

MMI's website published Ba'asyir's opinion and biography, and some pro-Ba'asyir cyber-activists also related his theory. Indeed, all the conspiracy theories surrounding the Bali bombing reflected the meta-narrative that the United States would always use any means to destroy Islam. E-mails questioning several coincidences (such why a U.S. State Department travel warning was issued several hours prior to the bombing, or why no American citizen had been killed in the blast) were circulated in Indonesian cyberspace. (In fact, several Americans had been killed.) There were also many Internet rumors about American involvement in this event—including one rumor suggesting that many Americans who frequented the bombed area had received SMS (short-message) warnings on their cellular phones to leave the area. This e-mail concluded that all "facts" pointed to U.S. involvement in the bombing.

The Bali bombing tragedy also brought out a new type of narrative construction that shared similar storylines and framing sentiments to earlier meta-narratives about the United States and Islam. Stories regarding the events of 9/11 and the Afghanistan invasion had originated from outside of Indonesia. These stories were situated in a global context of war against Islam and transported to Indonesia without much recontextualization or many local angles. But after the Bali bombing, the new narrative style married local Indonesian content and contexts to the radical meta-narrative of global dualism. Accounts and interpretations of subsequent related events (such as the Jakarta Marriot bombing in August 2003, the Australian embassy bombing in September 2004, and the bombing of the Indonesian embassy in Paris in October 2004) were now colored by many stories written in Indonesian by Indonesians. In other words, while these narratives were cooked in the same pot of global conspiracy against Islam, they were now composed of various local ingredients.

One active Indonesian Internet activist located in Banten, for example, has written several articles on his efforts to (a) link domestic (Indonesian) events with global events and to (b) locate the United States and Israel (specifically, the CIA and Mossad) as nodes that link all these

the Internet [is] a powerful tool to construct a new reality

disjointed occurrences. In his article—entitled *Legian, Kuta, Bali Bombing: Armagedon in Paradise—Mossad et CIA's Foolitrick?* (Jussac 2002)—he uses a plethora of selected Internet-based information to argue that the beneficiaries of the blast in Bali as well as the 9/11 tragedy were the "Cabals" (i.e., the shadow leaders in the United States). The author accused the FBI of planting an Indonesian identity card (*KTP, Kartu Tanda Penduduk*) at the bomb location in Bali as well as planting Saudi Arabian passports at the World Trade Center in New York. He also linked the travel warning of the U.S. embassy in Jakarta with the alleged pre-9/11 warning to 4,000 Israelis who worked in the WTC. And he argued that the type of explosive materials used in Bali could only have been owned by agents of Mossad, MI5, and the CIA. After providing many stories and linking together many names and places from different parts of the world and from different periods of time in his conspiracy theory, the author concluded that the Bali bombing demonstrated the intensification of hatred against Islam and the U.S.-Israel strategy to stigmatize Islam. This case clearly shows how strong a hold the meta-narrative of global conspiracy can have for some Indonesians. In this context, the

For Indonesian cyber-audiences, these…are "virtually" more powerful than CNN or BBC

Internet becomes a powerful tool in the construction of a new reality—a reality consisting of selected stories identified as "facts" and "truths" and stitched together with a larger explanation. Supported by the power of Internet networking, just a handful of Internet users who want to convince others of a global conspiracy against Islam can easily disseminate and share their belief and resistance identity to millions of other Indonesian users. For Indonesian cyber-audiences, these people are "virtually" more powerful than CNN or BBC.

Beyond Cyberspace

Beyond cyberspace, cyber-rumors of conspiracy also find a way to reach people who are not online. The major linkage in Indonesia is the print media, which are highly dependent on online sources. Islamist media, newspapers, and magazines—such as *Sabili, Republika, Suara Hidayatullah, Saksi,* and *Media Dakwah*—rely heavily on Islamic fundamentalist online sources. *Sabili* and *Suara Hidayatullah* (both also have associated websites) rely especially heavily on the Internet for their content. Narratives detailing a U.S.-Israel conspiracy spread quickly through these print media: The daily *Republika* published the e-mail headlined "4,000 Jews absent on the day of WTC attack" in its September 21, 2001 edition, and an Islamist mass circulation-magazine *Sabili* also published this story along with myriad other similar stories. *Republika* and other Islamist media cited mailing-list conspiracy theories as much as they did online sources such as Afghan Islamic Press, Islamic Online, and Al-Jazeera.

> *cyber-rumors of conspiracy also find a way to reach people who are not online*

It is important to note that, while mainstream publications such as *Kompas, Media Indonesia,* or *the Jakarta Post* may have higher circulations than the above publications, their readers are mostly concentrated in Jakarta and other big cities of Java. Readers of Islamist media, on the other hand, are widely spread across Indonesia, reaching even small villages in out-of-Java islands. *Sabili* and other Islamist media—such as *Suara Hidayatullah, Media Dakwah,* and *Salafy*—also have a more egalitarian strategy in circulating their products. These publications are not sold in upscale bookstores but through small kiosks where people buy cigarettes, in simple small Padang restaurants/cafes where people can buy a lunch for less than $1, and through street vendors. They are also sold by street kids at traffic junctions as well as at prayer gatherings in university campuses. In Jakarta, *Sabili* is sold at many kiosks in major bus stations. These Islamist print media are sometimes distributed freely at mosques and are also sold by small newspaper agents across the country. Forty agents in Jakarta, Surabaya, and Yogyakarta claim that *Sabili* is the most popular publication they offer. It is always sold out—not only because people like to buy it, but also because the publisher does not want any returns, so agents are occasionally forced to sell the magazine at a discount or even to give it away (Muhammad 2001).

Sabili—which, according to an AC Nielsen Survey, was the second-most-popular magazine in Indonesia—is even sold to a *madrasah* in a small village of Gunung Tembak in Borneo island (Kalimantan). This magazine can be found in one of the village's *Hidayatullah pesantren* (*Hidayatullah* is one of a number of Indonesia's networks of religious fundamentalist boarding schools, with 120 branch schools throughout the country). For students in these schools such as 16-year-old Muhammad

Fadhil, *Sabili* is the main source of current affairs. Fadhil says that he learned from the magazine that George Soros is a Hungarian Jew who runs the U.S. economy, that Bill Clinton was once governor of Arkansas and had an affair with Monica Lewinsky, and that 4,000 Jews who worked in the World Trade Center took a holiday on 9/11. Fadhil added that: "From the very deep of my heart, I think the United States is evil." Even more troubling, Fadhil and his friends—who admitted that sometimes they sneaked out of the *madrasah* to go to Internet cafes, where they logged onto both Laskar Jihad's website as well as the websites of popular American singers such as Britney Spears and soccer star Clint Mathis—said that they would like to join al-Qaeda if approached (Perlez 2002).

"From the very deep of my heart, I think the United States is evil."

With such wide distribution networks, Islamist media can play a central role in extending the dissemination of Internet-based information. After 9/11, these outlets became the main conduit for anti-Western Internet discourse to reach non-Internet users. It is thus not surprising to find low-income hawkers in peripheral areas of Bandung who talk about a conspiracy between Bush and Ariel Sharon to fight against Muslims:

> Unexpectedly, Americans now are known for their dirt. That
> President Bush apparently is a teammate of that Jewish Sharon! No
> doubt, all bombings were resulted from their conspiracy, to blame us,
> the Muslims (translated from Sundanese).[28]

Even local media that claim to be "secular" such as the daily newspaper *Pikiran-Rakyat* also follow the path of *Sabili* and *Republika*. *Pikiran-Rakyat* has published a considerable amount of anti-U.S.-Israel articles, some of which were heavily based on discussions on the Internet.

Besides these print media, Islamist book publishers also play a similar role in disseminating the conspiracy meta-narrative. Good examples of this trend are books about Osama bin Laden that have been published or reissued post-9/11: Titles include *Osama bin Laden Melawan Amerika* ("Osama bin Laden is against the United States") (Bashori 2000), a pre-9/11 title that was re-published after the attacks and sold very well. Other stated book themes that became more popular after 9/11 included "how to do *jihad*" or "the importance of *jihad,*" the U.S.-Israel conspiracy, the "Zionist-Crusader conspiracy" against Islam, the Palestine-Israel conflict, and the persecution of Muslims worldwide. All these books try to contextualize as well as justify *jihad* actions by giving readers the "absolute truth" of a Western conspiracy against Islam. They do not give space for any doubt and are written in an unambiguous way with black and white stories. Some of these books refer heavily to online sources, especially when dealing with global stories of Israel and U.S. conspiracy against Islam.

> *All these books… contextualize as well as justify jihad*

Some others, while not directly citing online sources nor directly related to Internet-based information, share the same spirit of *jihad.*

In addition to influencing books and other media for adult Muslims, the *jihad* concept has also become the main theme in many Islamic books for children. Comic books with heroic stories of holy wars and *mujahedeen* who fight the enemy in the name of Allah and with covers depicting a hero with a saber in his or her hand fill the racks of children's sections of bookstores in Jakarta and Bandung (see Figure 4). *Jihad*—in the form of physical war—has become a natural and daily part of conversation for Indonesian Muslims. These books may not necessarily intend to incite children to engage in *jihad.* But by showcasing their heroes and heroines as *jihadist* fighters instead of peacemakers—and recalling that the prophet Muhammad himself was a peacemaker—these titles tout violence and force as a means to solve perceived victimization and marginalization. Psychological research has shown that children who see media violence

Figure 4. Examples of Children's Books with *Jihad* Theme

Photo: Merlyna Lim

may become less sensitive to the pain and suffering of others, more fearful of the world around them, and more likely to behave in aggressive or harmful ways toward others (National Institute of Mental Health 1982). In other words, exposure to images and stories of *jihad* can be a seed for *jihadi* radicalism.

The Muted Third Voice

While it boosted the popularity of a U.S.-Israel conspiracy, the Bali bombing and subsequent bombings in Indonesia also increased Indonesian Muslim opposition to the *jihad*. That most of the bombings' victims were not identified with the "conspiracy," that many of those victims were Indonesians, and that the perpetrators proudly admitted their action after arrest—all these facts divided Indonesian Muslims in cyberspace into at least three groups. The first group still maintained that the United States and Israel were behind the Bali attack. The second group consists only a small number of hard-liners such as Abu Bakar Ba'asyir. While skeptical about Muslim involvement in the bombing, these hard-liners also think that a Muslim hand in the blast would have been an understandable reaction to what the United States was doing against Muslims all over the world and have failed only in not killing many Americans. The third group consists of those whom still believe there is a U.S.-Israel conspiracy against Muslims but who condemn the Bali bombing as a misleading use of the *jihad* concept worthy of punishment. While all three groups are present in cyberspace, voices from the last group—which actually consists of the majority of Muslims in Indonesia—seem to be underrepresented in both the Internet and in print media, domestically and internationally.

the Bali...and subsequent bombings... increased Indonesian Muslim opposition to the jihad

The Bali bombing also marked the distinct separation of conspiracy theories from the *jihad* concept. For radical fundamentalist groups such as Laskar Jihad, the *jihad* concept is always embedded in conspiracy theories. But the Bali bombing and subsequent arrests of Indonesians such as Imam Samudra (who declared that he did the bombing in the name of Islam and Allah) discredited widespread Indonesian belief in a pure Global *Jihad* meta-narrative. While most Indonesians believe in conspiracy theories pit-ﬞe West against Islam (van Bruinessen 2003, JIL 2003), this belief ﬞot mean that they also support *jihad*. Indeed, a survey done by LSI

(*Lembaga Survey Indonesia*) in 2004 shows that the majority of Indonesians believe in anti-Muslim conspiracy theories but do not have a real hatred towards Americans and thus cannot be considered capable of "killing for politics or religion."

In the nearly four years since 9/11 and the approximately three years since Laskar Jihad Online was closed down, the topic of a Western conspiracy against Islam is still popular among Indonesian Internet users and in the country's print media and daily conversations. But the majority of Indonesian Muslims are not extremists, and they reject Bin Ladenism, al-Qaeda, and the Taliban as a viable expression of what they believe. The Justice and Prosperity Party (PKS, *Partai Keadilan Sejahtera*) is an obvious example of this position. While many of its members and even its leaders believe in a U.S.-Israel anti-Muslim conspiracy, this Egyptian Muslim Brotherhood-oriented party—the most advanced Indonesian political party in the use of the Internet—does not encourage violence but instead promotes tolerance. The leaders and members of PKS promote themselves as democrats who are pluralist in forming coalitions; they also uphold high ethical standards in their public lives and promote their values through more than 20 PKS websites.

In fact, reformist Islamic groups in Indonesia are devoting much effort to a struggle against the growth of Indonesian radical fundamentalism and anti-Americanism. These reformists use the media—including the Internet—to spread a message of tolerance and peace, noting that Islam traditionally puts itself forward as a religion of peace. Nongovernmental organizations that promote interfaith dialogues and initiate reforms in Islam have emerged in Indonesia in the last half-decade. Among the most prominent ones is the *Jaringan Islam Liberal* (JIL, the Islam Liberal Network). JIL propagates its message through a website and mailing lists; it also collaborates with print publication and radio stations.

However, this nuanced "third voice" seems to be muted in Indonesian media discourse, defeated by the simplified message of *Salafy jihadism*. The JIL website (www.islamlib.com) is not as popular as fundamentalist websites, and the mailing list associated with JIL (islamliberal@yahoogroups.com) still has only around 500 members despite having been online for more than three years.[29] Articles published on the JIL website are cited mostly only in quality print media or media for elites—such as the *Jakarta Post*, *Kompas*, and *Tempo*—which, as noted previously, are not read by the majority of Indonesians. When these articles are cited in Islamist media, they are more often used to negate the JIL itself and to further buttress conspiracy theories and *jihad* meta-narrative.

JIL has been accused…
[of] being an
infidel…and part of
the Zionist-Crusader
conspiracy

In fact, JIL has been accused by radical fundamentalist groups of various offenses—being an infidel, a "CIA-agent," an American spy, pro-Zionist, and part of the Zionist-Crusader conspiracy—after it was discovered that the group had accepted funding from American-based organizations such as The Asia Foundation and the Ford Foundation. According to owners of the Pustaka Al-Kautsar, an online Islamic bookstore, the book *Menangkal Bahaya JIL & FLA* (Confining the Threat of JIL & FLA)—which basically claims that JIL's views are misleading and identifies JIL as Islam's chief enemy—is a bestseller. The bookstore's owners add that the book is more popular among Indonesians than the FLA's *Fiqih Lintas Agama*[30] (Paramadina 2003), a book that tries to popularize JIL's view. The electronic version of the anti-JIL book has become the most downloaded book of the collection of Swara Muslim, an online publisher.

Furthermore, the voices of moderate and tolerant Muslims in Indonesia are also subdued by the lack of nuance in U.S. foreign policy and U.S. insensitivity to the effects of its policies on the ground in the Muslim world. For example, in Indonesia, just as in any other part of the Muslim world, U.S. policies towards Palestine and in Israel are not seen as mutually supportive. The policy of the United States towards Israel is interpreted essentially as an anti-Muslim policy. In this manner, U.S. policies toward Jerusalem and the West Bank and Gaza have become indistinguishable for many Indonesian Muslims from the policies of Israel itself (Judge 1983). The Afghanistan invasion and (especially) the war in Iraq have strengthened this perception.

The Internet has played a specific and critical role in reinforcing these frustrations with U.S. policy by bringing the plight and suffering of fellow Muslims worldwide—especially those of Palestinians—closer to Indonesians. This exposure to international Muslim situations has accentuated many Indonesians' Islamic identity and religious solidarity. The Internet, television, and other means of communication have made these issues more personal. Since before 9/11 and on an almost daily basis, the Indonesian public has been flooded with audiovisual information about the Palestinian-Israeli conflict. The Internet and other media have enabled radical Islamic fundamentalist groups to capitalize on the sentiment of Muslim victimization by providing evocative texts and images of victimized Muslims from these conflicts. Images of dead bodies, blood, sorrowful Muslim women, and injured children are disseminated widely and with increasing frequency, provoking Muslims' anguish. Personified stories about *syuhada* (the Islamic martyr)

The Internet has played a specific and critical role in reinforcing…frustrations with U.S. policy

also embellish narratives of U.S.-Israel conspiracy, and somber Arabic songs and poems of angry Muslims such as the one below further provoke Muslim Internet surfers:

> Your cries, O beheaded babies… hit against the Palestine walls
> Your cries, O Afghan babies… waving to me without arms
> Executed by malicious bombs… of the evil American and its allies
> When your parents were going through Ramadhan!
>
> This is me, your brother…
> This is me, coming with a portion of a bomb…
> I will revenge your broken hearts…
> I will revenge your blood…
>
> Blood with blood…
> Body with body!…
> Qishash!!
> (Samudra 2004, translated from Indonesian)

For some Indonesian Muslims, regardless of their positions toward *jihad*, this poem by Imam Samudra—the Bali bomber—touches their soul with more than 100 lines of arguments by the U.S. government or the complicated views of the JIL.

What Have We Learned?

The two cases show how radical fundamentalist groups and individuals in Indonesia have used the Internet (in combination with other media) to disseminate their opinions and influence people's perceptions that

Muslims are the victims of an ongoing and growing Judeo-Christian hegemony. The following lessons can be drawn from the two cases.

Multiple Identities

The Internet appeals to isolated individuals by helping them to connect with people worldwide with whom they share some commonality. It also leads these individuals to spend more time with this de-territorialized community at the expense of interaction with their immediate physical environments. In cyberspace, communities are no longer tied to nations— a situation that corresponds to the mythical *umma* of *Salafism*, which specifically rejects nationalism and fosters the global *jihad* priority of fighting against the "far enemy" rather than the "near enemy." Dis-embedded from any territory, the vague establishment of an Islamist state must necessarily come into conflict with the only remaining political, economic, cultural, and military superpower—the United States. This reduces the project of the *umma* to a global Manichean fight with the United States for hegemony of the world in all these arenas—a true clash of civilizations.

However, people always have multiple identities. Indonesian Muslims correspond not only with their religious identity—as Muslim and a member of global *umma*—but also with their national identity. In the context of the rise of Islamic radicalism and the "war on terror" of the United States, Indonesian Muslims often alternate between these identities. Laskar Jihad, however, was able to connect both identities by rallying along religious *and* nationalism issues—a connection that added to the group's supremacy. Thus, for Indonesian Muslims in Java, far away from the Maluku Islands, the separatist movement in Maluku could simultaneously be both the enemy of the nation-state and the enemy of Islam—both the relatively nearer enemy and the far enemy. This dual identity also partially explains why the Maluku conflict incited the involvement of more Muslims in Java than did the conflicts in East Timor or Aceh.

The Socio-political Hierarchy, Old and New

The Internet has often transcended old hierarchies. It tremendously enhances the prospects for an egalitarian type of communications in which every voice is potentially as important as another. For Muslim Internet users, this capability opens space to examine religion with no authority except the texts of the Qur'an and Haditz. By learning from the Internet, people can feel they have acquired enough Islamic knowledge to guide important life decisions without having recourse to more traditional scholars such as an *imam* or Islamic teachers in local mosques. At the same time, radical fundamentalist groups can also use the Internet to bypass local authorities—national/sub-national authorities, an *imam*, local religious leaders, and parents—and directly reach ordinary Muslims in cyberspace.

However, simply because cyberspace transcends old hierarchies does not mean other hierarchies will not emerge there. In the case of Laskar Jihad, the Internet built social hierarchy by relying on a classic hierarchical form: the divine authority of a charismatic figure and his ability to consolidate legitimacy and generate obedience through and for religious faith. Laskar Jihad denounced the authority of Abdurrahman Wahid both as President and especially as a high leader of the Islamic community in Indonesia, allowing a new religious authority (made up of Saudi Arabian and Yemeni sheiks) that was not territoriality bound to emerge. In this case, the Internet was used not to remove hierarchy but to justify a new, de-territorialized pattern of hierarchy.

> *[although] cyberspace transcends old hierarchies, [it] does not [imply it is immune to new] hierarchies*

Reductionist Tendency, Simplified Message

The mass nature of the Internet also encourages sound bites and other reductionist answers to difficult questions. This quality plays into the argument of *Salafist* and other Islamic fundamentalist strains, which encourage extreme and simplistic solutions without regard to the reality and complexity of life. The simplified positions of *Salafy jihadism*, *Salafism*, and similar ideologies negate the sophistication of 14 centuries of commentaries on the Qur'an—commentaries that often include past responses to difficulties in the application of the Qur'an to contemporary problems. Fundamentalist messages, on the other hand, target not Islamic scholars but ordinary Muslims, some of whom are attracted by simplistic and direct theological reasoning. In this great contest for the soul of Muslim Internet surfers, the straightforwardness, simplicity, and clarity of *Salafy* types of ideology have no real competition. Both more traditional Islamic traditions and newer, more liberal wings of Islam are often seen as being far too complicated. *Salafist* rhetoric dominates Muslim Internet sites, most of which are created by Muslims who are living in the West (predominantly in the United States, Great Britain, and Canada) and who have immigrated, converted, or are temporarily studying there (Roy 2002: 165–83).

In addition, the conspiracy theories embedded in much of *Salafist* types of messages also have magnetic allure as simplified and easily digested explanations of local and world issues. Conspiracy theories throw responsibilities for all problems—unwanted, uncomfortable, and negative things—on somebody else's shoulder. Conspiracy-theory advocates and believers do not need to look at their own weaknesses nor mistakes and do not have to be introspective or criticize "the self": Every unwanted factor emanates from "the other." The reductionist tendency and simplicity of narratives of conspiracy and *Salafy jihadism* fit better with the mass nature of the Internet. It is thus understandable why this kind of message is even more popular in cyberspace than it is in other media.

Media Intermodality

The Internet network extends its influence by linking with other media and networks—including more traditional networks. These linkages are formed through intermodalities—the overlapped networks of various media; through them, information originating from cyberspace can flow beyond the computer screen and reach more audiences.

We must also consider other communication and information networks—those webs of interpersonal communication that do not operate through media, even though they are fed by and feed into media. These networks are essential both to media such as the Internet and radical movements. The notion of media audience implied by such networks is very different from a traditional one. Those members of the audience who are active in social networks during times of social tumult and political crisis are often the best-placed heralds of new media and the best-informed advisers on new-media movement strategies for those networks. In these audience members we can find the key communicative linkages between media and radical movements.

The case of Laskar Jihad demonstrates a particularly clear instance of how pre-existing media networks relate to the Internet as a core medium. The printed content of Laskar Jihad Online was circulated through communitarian social networks and religious networks, and the values and traditions of these established media networks gave cohesion, sanction, and energy to Laskar Jihad's vast anti-secular movement. To understand the role of the Internet in this movement, it is essential to examine how the movement's online content interacted with these established networks.

The Internet—A Global Trawling Tool?

Most *mujahedeen* in Maluku and worldwide were not recruited through the Internet, and not all funds for *jihad* were raised through the medium. Yet the role of the Internet and other related media used by *jihadi* groups should not be minimized. The Internet (and particularly its linkages to other media) has enabled the realization of new connections. It enables connections between radical groups and those individuals who have a pre-disposition to *jihad* and share the same ideology but were previously geo-graphically unreachable or socially isolated. The radical fundamentalist groups do not need the whole world to join the *jihad*; they only need to link with those who want to join them.

The following message, written by Imam Samudra and highlighted in both the print and online versions of his book,[31] demonstrates the impor-tance of the Internet to radical fundamentalist Islam:

> …, actually the main message I want to tell, especially to the young generation of Muslims, is that the knowledge of [internet] hacking and the reading of the Yellow book[32]—which mostly are seen as being antagonistic—should be mutually mastered or at least understood. It will be even better if you also have some understanding about bomb techniques or strategies in fighting and killing to be used for *jihad fis-abililah*. Therefore, as we are now in the Apocalypse days, please keep trying to be a preacher (*ustadz or da'i*), hacker, bomber and fighter or killer! (Samudra 2004: 5, translated from the Indonesian).

"Killing and Dying" for Religion

Imam Samudra's words demonstrate how the Internet can help bridge the gap from the isolated potential *mujahid* to any *jihad* organization. The Internet *is* undeniably useful for socializing a potential *mujahid* to the ide-ology of the global *jihad*. After 9/11, the Internet allowed many Muslims to become sensitized to Muslim issues and to develop a sense of collective social and resistance identity. And through the Internet, these potential *mujahid* could find out the address of organizations that (after vetting) might eventually help them link to the *jihad*.

However, the Internet does not provide a means to contact the *jihad* directly; nor does it allow the organization to assess the reliability of a potential candidate. There is no evidence that the Internet is persuasive enough by itself to elicit the type of allegiance that the *jihad* demands. *Jihad* in the form of physical war is not simply a blind and bloody-minded scramble for temporal power. Nor is it solely a door through which to pass into the hereafter. Rather, *jihad* is a form of political action in which the pursuit of immortality is inextricably linked to a profoundly this-worldly endeavor—the founding or recreation of a just community on earth (Arendt 1972).

There is also no convincing evidence that Laskar Jihad *mujahedeen* joined the *jihad* solely on the basis of what they had read on the Internet. Laskar Jihad did claim that some Muslim Internet users registered online to be *mujahedeen* and then joined its training camp, but it is unlikely that these recruits joined the cause solely because of the Internet alone. There is no evidence that one would go straight to an Afghan or Iraqi training camp from an Internet café.

Conclusion

The cases of Laskar Jihad and post-9/11 Islamic radicalism and anti-Americanism in Indonesia reveal that the Internet plays a critical yet ultimately indeterminate role in sociopolitical struggles. The Internet potentially can support individuals or groups who are or perceive themselves to be marginalized; it allows such groups to express their opinions and extend their influence. The two cases are exceptionally revealing examples of how the Internet can be used by a radical fundamentalist organization to reinforce its identity and ideologies, expand its network, and disseminate information and meanings. Both cases show that the Internet has allowed seemingly local events to be integrated into distantly managed networks. These networks use such local events to buttress and justify ideologies and agendas—ideologies and agendas that can be implemented when and where conditions are ripe. Cyberspace thus becomes a network of sites where groups in conflict extend their offline existence and power into localized confrontations that can entail violence.

the Internet plays a critical yet ultimately indeterminate role in sociopolitical struggles

Among the more powerful ways that cyberspace becomes divided into contested virtual and real spaces is through identity formation. As symbols, stylized messages, and news tailored to conform to religious and other identities coalesce around websites, mailing lists, and decision-making organizations operating through the Internet, conflict can be scaled down to local

Confrontations generated in even the most remote locale feed into a global identity

situations and scaled up into a global context. Confrontations generated in even the most remote locale feed into a global identity politics as evidence of conspiracy against the group.

The two cases show, however, that using the Internet is not persuasive enough to mobilize people for a *jihad* type of collective action. Internet distributive networks allow global meta-narratives to incite the local and the local to confirm the global. But in the end, a meta-narrative is always flawed in that it cannot ring true everywhere. In an archipelagic society as complex as Indonesia, "realities" of experiences vary too much to be consistent with the meta-narrative, even when—as with Laskar Jihad's meta-narratives—it combines nationalism and religion. The fact that most Indonesians did not join the *jihad*—not in Maluku, or in Afghanistan or Iraq—is evidence of a more hopeful society than that imagined by terrorism. As Reza Aslan (2005) points out in his book *No god but God: The Origins, Evolution, and Future of Islam*, the real objective of *jihad* fighters was for the soul and mind of Muslims, not to defeat the supposedly Neo-Crusaders. But these fighters failed because meta-narratives and conspiracies are too vague to encompass all experiences and killing is not a universally shared response to distant episodes. As Aslan (2005) says, the emergence of *jihad* fighters is possibly a sign of weakness and ultimate collapse—not a sign of ascendancy or universal truth.

Endnotes

1. This article is based on the author's research funded by WOTRO/NWO (The Netherlands) and subsequent research funded by the East-West Center Washington and The Henry Luce Foundation. The manuscript was written during the author's three-months residence in Washington, D.C. as a Southeast Asia visiting fellow at the East-West Center Washington. All translations from Indonesian and Sudanese were done by the author.

2. The word "*jihad*" (*Ju-h-D*) means "effort," "struggle," or "striving." In its primary sense *jihad* is an inner thing, within a self, to rid that self from debased actions or inclinations and exercise constancy and perseverance in achieving a higher moral standard. In this monograph, *jihad* is used to speak to a form of a physical war against the "unfaithful." In recent history, the notion of *jihad* in the form of violence—as it is used in this monograph—is predominant; it is a common word used by "resistance, liberation and terrorist movement alike to legitimizate their cause and motivate their followers" (Esposito 2002: 26).

3. *Mujahedeen*—or also transliterated *as mujahideen, mujahedin, mujahidin, mujaheddin,* etc.—literally translates from Arabic as "strugglers." *Mujahid* means "struggler." The root of the word *mujahedeen* is *Ju-h-D* or *jihad*. *Mujahid* is therefore someone who exerts effort or struggles; *mujahedeen* is simply the plural. While the word has been extensively use in the context of "holy war," there is no explicit "holy" or "warrior" within the word itself.

4. The author regularly visited various websites and mailing lists listed in Appendices 1 and 2. Some of the mailing lists have their archives available for public; some do not. To access archives that are not available for public, the author subscribed as a (passive) member of those mailing lists.

5. In his speech on Independence Day, August 17, 1951, Sukarno rationalized the use of force against South Maluku because RMS did not welcome the peaceful efforts

Indonesia had initiated (Sukarno in Puar 1956: 8–9). By blaming those whom he termed "disloyal separatists," Sukarno tried to suppress the voices of federalism at that moment who had pointed out that the government's effort in uniting Indonesia was more of a forced action than a strategic effort (Sunday Couriers 1950).

6. The major history books for the third grade of junior high school (or ninth grade) in the 1975 to 1994 curricula clearly mentioned RMS as one of most important separatist movements in the history of the Republic of Indonesia. The relatively significant change in the interpretation of RMS happened after the 1998 political reform, when many stories (especially about separatism and rebellion movements) in school history books were revised (Depdikbud 1999). In more recent history books, these events are described as just events without any tendency to inscribe overwhelmingly negative judgments. Until early 2003, all elementary schools and junior high schools in Indonesia could use only those books approved by the government's Department of Education and Culture (which in 2004 became the Department of National Education) for major sources of teaching. In early 2003, the Department endorsed the rule that allowed schools to choose their curricular books by themselves.

7. All history books of the Maluku published by the Department of Education and Culture (except the latest book) mentioned this fact. The latest version states that, while the North of Maluku (especially Ternate and Tidore) had been in touch with Islam before Portuguese brought Christianity, the South of Maluku (Uliase, Ambon, Buru, and Seram) were actually never touched by Islam. The religion of indigenous people there was animism or the so-called "pre-Islamic belief" (Depdikbud 1999).

8. The phrase *tabligh akbar* (Arabic) comes from two words; *tabligh* and *akbar*. Tabligh literally means "the propagation of message," while *akbar* literally means "big, grand, great." The original purpose of *tabligh* is to disseminate the message of Allah faithfully in its true form, fully and completely.

9. The word *salafy* comes from *salaf*. *Salaf* literally means "those (from history) who precede, have gone before." *Salafy* means "of the *salaf*." The "i" or "y" (which sounds like "ee") on the end of the word means "of the," "of," and/or "are." The word *salafy* can only be used in association with words that are of things that are truly from the distant past. In this case (when referring to Islamic matters) it refers to things that are from the first three generation of pious Muslims or from those who came after them but who are still considered in the distant past to us today.

10. It is important to differ *Salafy Jihadism* from *Salafism*. While both share a similar determination to restore the purity of the faith and regard themselves as guardians of that purity, they differ in four issues. "One, as is whether it is permissible to rebel against Muslim governments. *Salafis* say no, *salafy jihadis* say yes. A second is on organization. *Salafy jihadis* in order to achieve their political goals, need a level of organization that to *salafy* purists, smacks on 'partyism.' *Salafis* then to define the concept of *jihad* in broad terms as the taking of whatever actions are necessary to improve one's own faith; *salafy jihadi* define it as battle. Finally they differ on tactics and acceptable methodology for achieving their aims, particularly with respect to *jihad*" (ICG 2004: 29).

11. Thalib claimed that Laskar Jihad consisted of about 40,000 members and several hundred thousand supporters.

12. Among these books are *Thalib* (2001a) and *Kastor* (2000a, 2000b, 2000c).

13. Taken from an Islamic teenage chatroom, recorded on August 19, 2002.

14. As of October 2001, there were 1,419 members on this mailing list.

15. Calling PDI-P "Christian-Nationalist" is not without reason. Undeniably 53 out of 153 members of Parliament (MPs) from PDI-P were Christians (Catholic and Protestant), and all PDI-P MPs from the Maluku were Christians.

16. SPPM: *Suara Perjuangan Muslim Maluku* (The Voice of Muslims' Struggles in the Maluku). This radio program was aired in the Maluku and owned by FKAJW.

17. For example: http://listen.to/ambon, http://scroll.to/ambon, http://connect.to/Maluku, and http://come.to/ suaraambon.

18. There are not many Indonesian Christian websites compared with the number of Muslim ones. While there are some Christian websites on the Maluku conflicts, these websites were not necessarily linked to the regular Christian websites but mostly linked to each other.

19. For example: www.alsofwah.or.id/html/berita.html, www.malu.ku.org/, www.ummah.net/, sos/indonesia.htm., and http://islamic-world.net/youth/jihadambon&aceh.htm.

20. The observation of *Republika*'s reporting news on the Maluku conflict before the launch of the Laskar Jihad Online is based on an unpublished master's thesis written by Buni Yani (2002).

21. See Abbas and Pakkanna (2000), Ahmad and Oesman (2000), Djaelani (2001), and Kastor (2000a, 2000b, 2000c).

22. For comparison, the total national circulation of print media in Indonesia in 2001 was less than 2 million (as stated by President Abdurahman Wahid) or less than 1.5 million in 1999 (according to the National Socio-Economic Survey). This number is shared by approximately 1,500 print media outlets, making for an average circulation of only 1,000 exemplars per outlet. Only well established national print media like *Kompas, Suara Pembaruan*, and *Media Indonesia* have total circulation of more than 100,000 exemplars; most of new print media start with circulation of less than 20,000 exemplars.

23. These interviews (in the form of informal conversation) were conducted in July and August 2002. The interviewees (randomly selected) were Muslim: 10 male and six female students ages 18–39 and in educational situations ranging from high school to Ph.D. student. All were Internet users and all of them had accessed Laskar Jihad Online and received information originated from Laskar Jihad.

24. Posted on Sept. 12, 2001, at daarut_tauhid@yahoogroups.com. The mailing list's archive was available for public on this date. It was no longer available as of October 2004 and remains closed to the public.

25. See appendix 1.

26. The Laskar Jihad officially stated in its press conference that Osama bin Laden did not finance their *jihad* movement in Maluku (FKAWJ September 22, 2001).

27. Research on 9/11 coverage in Indonesian print media and TV by Eriyanto and Pontoh (2001) shows a similar tendency. The researchers discovered that Indonesian media found it difficult to maintain balanced views. These media also aped the Taliban's and bin Laden's claim that the United States was making war against Islam.

The Indonesian media short-circuited objections from Muslim audiences by publishing news captured from the anti-U.S. frame of the Taliban and bin Laden. The country's Islamist media took a very radical view by referring only explanations and narratives of Taliban government.

28. Personal interview, August 15, 2002.

29. One can argue that this mailing list does not have a great number of participants because someone needs a moderator's approval to become a member. However, some fundamentalist-based mailing lists that apply a similar rule are still much more popular than JIL mailing lists.

30. The term *fiqih* or *fikh* can be translated as Islamic jurisprudence. *Fiqih Lintas Agama* can be translated as "Cross-Religion Fikh," the first step to formulating a dialogical *fikh* compromise with other religions. Such a move is an attempt to deconstruct and reconstruct the classical *fikh* (Gazali 2003). Most Muslims believe that the *fikh* produced by the Islamic leaders in the golden age of Islam can solve all contemporary issues. Indonesian reformists at the Islam Liberal Network, however, believe that *fikh* is a dynamic intellectual product of a certain time and context and therefore could and should be interpreted to fit Indonesia's contemporary socio-cultural-political context.

31. Imam Samudra's book *Aku Melawan Teroris* (I Fight against the Terrorist) was written in jail while he was awaiting trial. Published in September 2004, its first edition (3,000 copies) sold out in a week. The publisher now is working on a second edition. The electronic version of this book is also online, though it is not yet fully finished.

32. The Yellow Book (*kitab kuning*) refers to books used to study the religion (Islam) that contain classical texts of the various Islamic disciplines as well as commentaries, glosses, and supercommentaries on basic texts written over the ages. "The corpus of classical texts accepted in the *pesantren* tradition—in theory at least—are conceptually closed; the relevant knowledge is thought to be a finite and bounded body. Although new works within the tradition continue to be written, these have to remain within strict boundaries and cannot pretend to offer more than summaries, explications or rearrangements of the same, unchangeable, body of knowledge…In practice, however, the tradition appears to be much more flexible than the above sketch would suggest" (Van Bruinnesen, 1994: 121).

Bibliography

Abbas, Nurdin and Mukhaer Pakkanna. 2000. *Bara di Maluku: Upaya Untuk Mempertahankan Sejengkal Tanah.* Jakarta: Yayasan Lukman Harun.

Ahmad, Kasman Hi and Herman Oesman. 2000. *Damai Yang Terkoyak: Catatan Kelam dari Bumi Halmahera.* Ternate: Madani Press.

Apadurrai, Arjun. 1996. *Modernity at Large: Cultural Dimensions of Globalization.* Minneapolis: University of Minnesota Press.

Arendt, Hannah. 1972. *Crises on the Republic.* New York: Harcourt Brace & Co.

Aslan, Reza. 2005. *No god but God: The Origins, Evolution, and Future of Islam.* New York: Random House.

Bashori, Ahmad Dhumyathi. 2000. *Osama bin Laden Melawan Amerika.* Bandung: Mizan.

Beck, Ulrich. 2000. "The Cosmopolitan Perspective: sociology of the second age of modernity." *British Journal of Sociology* 51(1): 79–107.

Bräuchler, Birgit. 2003. "Cyberidentities at War: Religion, Identity, and the Internet in the Moluccan Conflict." *Indonesia* 75: 123–51.

Bush, George W. 2001. "Text of President Bush's Statement Wednesday." Accessed at http://multimedia.belointeractive.com/attack/news/0912bushstatement.html (text) and www.whitehouse.gov/news/releases/2001/09/20010912-4.v.smil (audio), on Sept. 12, 2001.

Castells, Manuel. 1997. *The Power of Identity: The Information Age–Economy, Society and Culture.* Cambridge, MA & Oxford: Blackwell.

Depdikbud. 1977. *Sejarah Daerah Maluku.* Jakarta: Departemen Pendidikan dan Kebudayaan RI.

_____. 1983a. *Sejarah Sosial di Daerah Maluku*. Jakarta: Departemen Pendidikan dan Kebudayaan RI.

_____. 1999. *Sejarah Maluku*. Jakarta: Departemen Pendidikan dan Kebudayaan RI.

Diani, Mario. 2000. "Social Movement Networks Virtual and Real." *Information, Communication & Society* 3(3): 386–401.

Djaelani, Abdul Kadir. 2001. *Agama dan separatisme menjadi landasan konflik Maluku dan Poso*. Jakarta: Yayasan Pengkajian Islam Madinah Al-Munawwarah.

Ebiz Asia. 2001. "Life in Days After September 11 Terrorist Strikes." Transcript of interviews aired on October 6, 2001, a weekly TV show broadcast by CNN International.

Eriyanto and Andreas Harsono. 2001. "Bali, Terrorism, and the Indonesian Media." In *Journalism Asia: Media and Terrorism*, Manila: Center for Media Freedom and Responsibility.

Esposito, John. 2002. *Unholy War, Terror in the Name of Islam*. Oxford: Oxford University Press.

Faksh, Mahmud A. 1997. *Fundamentalism in Egypt, Algeria and Saudi Arabia*. London: Praeger.

FKAWJ. 2002. "Ustadz Ja"far Umar Thalib: Rencana intervensi militer AS, upaya penghancuran umat Islam." Accessed at www.laskarjihad.or.id, on July 30, 2002.

Foucault, Michel. 1972. *The Archeology of Knowledge & The Discourse on Language*. New York: Pantheon Books.

Freeman, Jo. 1979. "Resource Mobilization and Strategy: A Model for Analyzing Social Movement Organization Actions." In Mayer N. Zald and John D. McCarthy, eds., *The Dynamic of Social Movements: Resource Mobilization, Social Control, and Tactics*. Cambridge: Winthrop Publishers.

Freeman, L.C. 1999. "Visualizing Social Networks." Accessed at www2.heinz.cmu.edu/project/INSNA/joss/vsn.html, on Oct. 30, 2004.

Friedman, Jonathan. 1994. *Cultural Identity and Global Process*. London: Sage.

Gazali, Hatim. 2003. "Religion in new print." *Islam Liberal Network*. Accessed at http://islamlib.com/en/page.php?page=article&mode=print&id=540, on Nov. 6, 2004.

Goffman, E. 1974. *Frame Analysis*. New York: Harper Colophon.

Hall, Stuart. 1992. "The Question of Cultural Identity." In Stuart Hall, David Held, and Tony McGrew, eds., *Modernity and Its Futures* (pages 273–326). Cambridge: Polity Press.

Hasan, Noorhaidi. 2001. "Islamic Radicalism and the Crisis of the Nation-state." *ISIM Newsletter* 7 (March).

Hefner, Robert. 2003. "Civic Pluralism Denied? The New Media and *Jihadi* Violence in Indonesia." In Dale F. Eickelman and Jon W. Anderson, eds., *New Media in the Muslim World: The Emerging Public Sphere*. Bloomington: Indiana University Press.

Hidayatullah 2002. "Ayip Syarifuddin: Sang arsitek Laskar Jihad." Accessed at www.hidayatullah.com/2002/04/profil.shtml, on April 20, 2003.

Hjarvard, Stig. 2002. "Mediated Encounters: An Essay on the Role of Communication Media in the Creation of Trust in the 'Global Metropolis.'" In Gitte Stald and Thomas Tufte, eds., *Global Encounters: Media and Cultural Transformation* (pages 69–84). Luton: University of Luton Press.

Huntington, Samuel P. 1993. "The Clash of Civilizations." *Foreign Affairs* 73(3): 22–49.

ICG. 2000. *Indonesia: Overcoming Murder and Violence in Maluku.* Jakarta/Brussels, December 19.

_____. 2001. *Indonesia: Violence and Radical Muslims.* Jakarta/Brussels, October 10.

_____. 2002. *Indonesia: The Search for Peace in Maluku.* Jakarta/Brussels, February 8.

_____. 2004. *Indonesia Backgrounder: Why Salafism and Terrorism Mostly Don't Mix.* Asia Report No 83. Southeast Asia/Brussels, September 13.

Illich, Ivan (1973). *Tools for Conviviality.* London: Calder & Boyars.

JIL (Islam Liberal Network). 2003. "Teori konspirasi selalu meneror kebenaran." Accessed at http://islamlib.com/id/page.php?page=article&id=414, on Oct. 20, 2004.

Judge, Joseph. 1983. "This Year in Jerusalem." *National Geographic* 163, No. 4 (April): 478–515.

Jussac, Yusuf bin. 2002. "Legian, Kuta, Bali Bombing: Armagedon in paradise—Mossad et CIA's Foolitrick." Accessed at www.dataphone.se/~ahmad/021016a.htm, on Oct. 31, 2004.

Kastor, Rustam. 2000a. *Fakta, Data dan Analisa: Konspirasi Politik RMS dan Kristen Menghancurkan Ummat Islam di Ambon-Maluku.* Yogyakarta: Wihdah Press. Accessed at www.geocities.com/r_kastor/Rustam-Isi.html, on Nov. 6, 2004.

_____. 2000b. *Suara Maluku Membantah, Rustam Kastor Menjawab,* Yogyakarta: Wihdah Press.

_____. 2000c. *Damai Sekarang atau Perang Berlanjut.* Yogyakarta: Wihdah Press.

Lim, Merlyna 2002. "Cyber-civic Space in Indonesia: From Panopticon to Pandemonium?" *International Development Planning Review* 24(4): 383–400.

_____. 2003a. "From *Warnet* to Netwar: The Internet and Resistance Identities in Indonesia." *International Information and Library Review* 35 (2–4): 233–48.

_____. 2003b. "The Internet, Social Network, and Reform in Indonesia." In Nick Couldry and Danny Miller, eds., *Contesting Media Power: Towards a Global Comparative Perspective* (pages 273–88). Lanham: Rowan and Littlefield.

_____. 2004. "The Polarization of Identity through the Internet and the Struggle for Democracy in Indonesia." *Electronic Journal of Communication/La Revue Electronique de Communication* 14 (3–4), accessed at www.cios.org/www/ejc-main.htm.

Lyotard, Jean-Francois. 1986. *The Postmodern Condition: A Report on Knowledge* (translated by Geoff Bennington and Brian Massum). Manchester: Manchester University Press.

Media Dakwah. 1999. "Perang Jihad masih berlanjut di Ambon." *Media Dakwah,* December.

Morley, David. 1999. "Transnationalism, feminism, and fundamentalism." In Caren Kaplan, Norma Alarcon and Minoo Moallem, eds., *Between Woman and Nation: Nationalism, Transnationalism, Feminism, and the State* (pages 320–28). London: Duke University Press.

Muhammad, Agus. 2001. "*Jihad* lewat tulisan." *Pantau,* 015(II), July. Accessed at www.pantau.or.id/txtx/15/06a.html.

Munindo. 2002. "Maklumat Laskar Jihad." Accessed at www.munindo.brd.de/artikel/artikel_04/art04_maklumat_laskar_jihad.html, on April 1, 2003.

National Institute of Mental Health. 1982. *Television and Behavior: Ten Years of Scientific Progress and Implications for the Eighties,* Volume 1. Rockville, MD: U.S. Department of Health and Human Services.

Ohorella, G. A., S. P. Harjono, and T. Wulandari. 1993. *Tantangan and Rongrongan Terhadap Keutuhan Negara and Kesatuan RI: Kasus Republik Maluku Selatan.* Jakarta: Depdikbud.

Orwell, George. 1954. *Nineteen Eighty-four.* Harmondsworth: Penguin Books.

Paramadina. 2003. *Fiqih Lintas Agama.* Jakarta: Paramadina.

Perlez, Jane. 2002. "The Impact Outside the Middle East." *Middle East Roundtable* 15(2), April 22.

Primamorista, Agung. 2001. "Amerika, Terrorisme, dan Zionisme." Accessed at www.era-muslim.com/article/view/6226.html, on Oct. 30, 2001.

Puar, Jusuf A. 1956. *Peristiwa Republik Maluku Selatan.* Jakarta: Penerbit Bulan-Bintang.

Roy, Olivier. 2002. *L'Islam Mondialisé.* Paris: Editions du Seuil.

Sabili. 1999a. "Moslem Cleansing, Ambon Tidak Sendirian." *Sabili* VI(3), March 29.

_____. 1999b. "Kristenisasi Jilid Dua." *Sabili* VII(3), July 28.

_____. 2000. "Memperingati Satu Tahun Tragedi Maluku Berdarah." *Sabili* XVI(16), Jan. 26.

Samudra, Imam. 2004. *Aku Melawan Teroris.* Solo: Jazera. Accessed at http://mcb.swara-muslim.net/index.php?section=23&page=-1, on Nov. 6, 2004.

Schulze, Kirsten E. 2002. "Laskar Jihad and the Conflict in Ambon." *Brown Journal of World Affairs* 9(1): 57–69.

Slevin, James. 2000. *The Internet and Society.* Cambridge: Polity Press.

Snow, David A. and Robert D. Benford 1988. "Ideology, Frame Resonance, and Participant Mobilization." *International Social Movement Research* 1: 197–217.

Suara Hidayatullah. 1999. "Membongkar Prakter GGG: Gold-Glory-Gospel: The Moslem Cleansing in Ambon." *Suara Hidayatullah,* October.

Sunday Couriers. 1950. Jakarta, April 30.

Tempo. 2002. "Hamzah Haz: Saya selalu akomodatif." Accessed at www.tempo.co.id/harian/wawancara/waw-hamzahhaz.html, on April 20, 2003.

Thalib, Ja'far Umar. 2001a. *Laskar Jihad Ahlus Sunnah wal Jamaah - Mempelopori perlawanan terhadap kedurjanaan hegemoni Salibis-Zionis internasional di Indonesia.* Yogyakarta: FKAWJ.

_____. 2001b. "Mampuslah Amerika." *Buletin Laskar Jihad 10.*

Turkle, Sherry. 1996. *Life on the Screen: Identity in the Age of the Internet.* London: Weidenfeld and Nicholson.

Van Bruinessen, Martin. 1994. "*Pesantren* and *kitab kuning*: Maintenance and Continuation of a Tradition of Religious Learning." In Wolfgang Marschall, ed., *Texts from the Islands: Oral and Written Traditions of Indonesia and the Malay World [Ethnologica Bernica, 4]* 1210145. Berne: University of Berne.

_____. 2003. "Post-Suharto Muslim Engagements with Civil Society and Democracy." Paper presented at the Third International Conference and Workshop "Indonesia in Transition," Universitas Indonesia Depok, August 24–28.

Yani, Buni. 2002. "Reporting the Maluku Sectarian Conflict: The Politics of Editorship in Kompas and Republika Dailies." Unpublished master thesis, Center for Southeast Asian Studies, Ohio University at Athens.

Appendix 1

List of Observed Mailing Lists

daarut-tauhiid@yahoogroups.com
fikrah@yahoogroups.com
hidayatullahnews@yahoogroups.com
is-lam@isnet.org
islam-liberal@yahoogroups.com
keadilan4all@yahoogroups.com
kmnu2000@yahoogroups.com
laskarjihad@yahoogroups.com
majelismuda@yahoogroups.com
msanews-list@yahoogroups.com
myquran@yahoogroups.com
sabili@yahoogroups.com
salafi-indonesia@yahoogroups.com

Appendix 2

List of Observed Websites

(urls of personal websites are not included)
http://islamic-world.net/youth/jihad ambon&aceh.htm
http://media.isnet.org
http://perangsalib01.cjb.net
http://walisongo.homestead.com/fpi.html
www.alislam.or.id
www.alsofwah.or.id/html/berita.html
http://www.ar-risalah.com
www.dataphone.se/~ahmad
www.hidayatullah.net
www.islamonline.net
www.islib.com
www.laskarjihad.or.id
www.malu.ku.org/
www.mujahidin.or.id
www.sabili.or.id
www.salafy.net
www.salafy.or.id
www.salafyoon.net
www.swaramuslim.net
www.ukhuwah.or.id
www.ummah.net/sos

Program Information

The Southeast Asia Fellowship Program
Purpose

The Southeast Asia Fellowship Program is designed to offer young scholars from Southeast Asia the opportunity to undertake serious academic writing on the management of internal and international conflicts in the region and to contribute to the development of Southeast Asian studies in the Washington area by bringing Asian voices to bear on issues of interest to a Washington audience.

The annual fellowships are awarded to two to three scholars and will finance two to three months of fieldwork in Southeast Asia, two months of residence at the Institute of Southeast Asian Studies, Singapore, and three months of residence at the East-West Center Washington in Washington, D.C. During the period in residence, the primary goal of the fellows is to complete a monograph or article that can be published in a peer-reviewed outlet. Fellows will also give seminars sponsored by the East-West Center Washington, partake in Southeast Asia related scholarly activities organized by other institutions, and interact with scholars and policy makers in Singapore and Washington, D.C.

Funding Support

This program is funded by a generous grant from The Henry Luce Foundation, Inc., with additional support from the Institute of Southeast Asian Studies, Singapore, and the East-West Center.

2004 Fellows

Evelyn Goh
Institute of Defence and Strategic Studies, Nanyang Technological University, Singapore

Herman Kraft
University of the Philippines, Diliman, Philippines

Merlyna Lim
Bandung Institute of Technology, Indonesia

2005 Fellows

Joseph Chinyong Liow
Institute of Defence and Strategic Studies, Nanyang Technological University, Singapore

Chandra-nuj Mahakanjana
National Institute of Development Administration, Thailand